the **13**

most important

BIBLE
LESSONS

for teenagers

COMPLETE MEETINGS FOR YOUTH GROUPS AND SUNDAY SCHOOL

Group

The 13 Most Important Bible Lessons for Teenagers:
Complete Meetings for Youth Groups and Sunday Schools

Copyright © 2015 Group Publishing, Inc. / 0000 0001 0362 4853

This book was formerly titled *Active Meetings on Basic Christianity* and first printed by Group Publishing in 1991.

group.com
simplyyouthministry.com

CREDITS
Originally Edited by Michael D. Warden
Revisions Edited by Stephanie Martin and Rick Lawrence
Designed by Veronica Preston
Cover design by Veronica Preston
Illustrations by Judy Atwood Bienick

Scripture quotations are from the HOLY BIBLE, NEW INTERNATIONAL VERSION ®. Copyright © 1973, 1978, 1984 by International Bible Society. Used by permission of Zondervan Publishing House. All rights reserved.

ISBN 978-1-4707-3370-4

12 11 10 9 8   24 23 22 21 20

Printed in the United States of America.

TABLE OF CONTENTS

Introduction 1

Lesson 1: Who Is Jesus? 3
Help teenagers see Jesus as the central focus of their lives.

Lesson 2: Who Is God? 13
Help young people get in touch with the heart of God.

Lesson 3: Who Is the Holy Spirit? 21
Guide students to recognize the Holy Spirit's power and work in their lives.

Lesson 4: What Is the Bible? 31
Explore how the Bible can impact teenagers' everyday lives.

Lesson 5: In the Beginning 41
Dive into what the Bible says about creation.

Lesson 6: The Human Journey 49
Learn what the Bible says about human nature.

Lesson 7: Why Does Life Hurt? 61
Help students understand why sin, evil, and suffering exist in the world.

Lesson 8: Family of Faith .67
Explore the importance of a growing relationship with Jesus.

Lesson 9: Why the Church? 79
Show teenagers how they can be vital members of God's church.

Lesson 10: Prayer Power! .85
Help young people grow in their understanding and practice of prayer.

Lesson 11: Sharing Jesus .95
Help students effectively influence others toward a relationship with Jesus.

Lesson 12: Faith in Action 103
Encourage teenagers to live out their faith practically through serving others.

Lesson 13: Eternity With Jesus 111
Discover what the Bible says about future events and eternity.

INTRODUCTION

"Why did Jesus die on the cross, anyway?" Jenna finally voiced the question that most of the other students were thinking. "I mean, why didn't God just wipe out sin and suffering? It doesn't make sense."

The youth leader suddenly realized she'd been speaking over students' heads. She'd been talking about Jesus' final words on the cross, but some of her students weren't even sure who Jesus is. And they didn't understand why an all-powerful, merciful God would allow his only Son to be brutally killed.

The leader needed to refocus her lesson—and the next several lessons—to teach her students the basics:

- **Who is Jesus?**
- **Who is God?**
- **What's a faith commitment?**
- **What's the church?**
- **Why do we need a Savior?**

Young people need a firm faith foundation to stand in the midst of challenging influences and competing "truths" in life. They need to know what they believe and why they believe it. Otherwise, they can be easily swayed by others who challenge their faith or lead them into an imitation Christianity.

But many teenagers don't have a strong faith foundation. Even students who've grown up in the church sometimes can't explain who Jesus is or what it means to be a Christian.

So how do you cover faith "basics" and still keep your lessons interesting and fun so young people will really learn?

Use *The 13 Most Important Bible Lessons for Teenagers!* These lessons cover 13 foundational doctrines of Christianity, without boring lectures and endless note-taking. By using R.E.A.L. (Relational, Experiential, Applicable, Learner-Based) techniques, these fun lessons will hold students' interest. Students will find it easy to learn about important Christian doctrines, such as:

- the power of Jesus' death and resurrection,
- the Holy Spirit's role in their life,
- the beauty and necessity of prayer, and
- the privilege of telling others about a relationship with Jesus.

The lessons also provide a biblical perspective on issues such as Creation and Jesus' return. And with fast instructions and easy-to-use handouts, you can help students learn these vital concepts with ease.

Use these lessons as Sunday school curriculum. Or plan a series of weekly Bible studies that focus on a different topic each week. The lessons work especially well for a confirmation class or a course for new Christians.

You can also cover certain topics as needs arise in your youth group. For example, in the scene described at the beginning of the Introduction, the youth leader could use three lessons: "Who Is Jesus?" "Who Is God?" and "The Family of Faith." Each provides valuable information about Jesus' identity and his mission here on earth.

As you explore these lessons, watch students' faith blossom as they build a foundation in Jesus that will last forever

WHO IS JESUS?

By Cindy Hansen

Who is Jesus, anyway? How do you define him for teenagers who have little knowledge of the Bible or the Christian faith? Well, Jesus isn't merely ...

- A super-nice guy.
- A great teacher and prophet.
- A good man who helped a lot of people, so we should model our lives after him.
- A mysterious guy who most people don't really understand but still talk about today anyway.

All these descriptions of Jesus way-underestimate him—and students need a true understanding of the God-man at the center of the Christian faith.

Use this lesson to teach young people about who Jesus is, what he did, and why he's so important to our everyday life.

OBJECTIVES

In this lesson, students will:

- explore what they already know about Jesus,
- search the Bible for descriptions and insights about Jesus,
- use "If ... then" statements to make connections to their lives today,
- design wanted posters of themselves, and
- receive a reminder of Jesus' love for them.

THE LESSON

Wanted—a Definition of Jesus

You'll need a copy of the "Wanted" poster on page 9, enlarged to 11×17 inches if possible. Tape the poster to a wall. For each person, you'll need a pencil and two large sticky notes.

As students enter the meeting room, give them each a pencil and two large sticky notes. Show the "Wanted" poster, and have students each write on their labels what they already know about Jesus. It can be as simple as "He was a man" or "He lived a long time ago."

After students have written their answers and stuck them to the poster, read their statements aloud. Say: **We're going to add to what we already know about Jesus and make connections to our lives today. We're all "private eyes" in search of a most-wanted man: Jesus.**

Mystery Theater

You'll need a Bible, a manger or a box labeled "Manger" that's filled with hay or straw, and as many of the following Sherlock Holmes props as you can get: a hat, a trench coat, a pipe, and a magnifying glass.

Put on the Sherlock Holmes outfit and walk over to the manger. In your best British accent, say: **Welcome to Mystery Theater. We're in search of a most-wanted man: a man named Jesus. But what do we know about this person? How do we solve the case of his true identity? Let's look at what we already know about Jesus' birth and early years.**

1. Jesus' mother was the Virgin Mary, and his earthly father was Joseph. Jesus is God's Son. You can read about those amazing facts in Luke 1:26-35.

2. Jesus was born in a small town called Bethlehem. He was born in a manger like this, because there wasn't room for his parents to stay in any of the town's inns (Luke 2:1-7).

3. Angels and a star led shepherds and wise men to see the baby Jesus. They'd been waiting for this amazing moment. Prophets from ages before had predicted Jesus' birth (Matthew 2:1-12 and Luke 2:8-20).

4. At age 12, Jesus astonished religious teachers in the temple with his knowledge about God (Luke 2:41-52).

5. Jesus began his ministry when he was about 30 years old (Luke 3:23).

Say: And here ends our Mystery Theater. Let's continue our search for other clues to this man's identity.

Jesus Clues

(For every two people, you'll need a Bible, a marker, and a copy of the "Clue Search" handout on page 10.)

Form pairs by having students, one at a time, say either "Sherlock" or "Watson." Have the Sherlocks each find a Watson for a partner.

Give each mystery-solving duo a Bible, a marker, and a "Clue Search" handout. Tell pairs the clues they'll analyze are found in the Bible. If students are unfamiliar with the Bible, have everyone use the same translation, and give students the page numbers where their verses are found.

Have pairs each look up one or more of the following Bible passages and write at least one fact about Jesus on their handout. Depending on the number of students you have, you may need to give more than one passage to each pair so all the passages are covered.

Here are the passages and clues:

- **Matthew 2:4-6 (Prophets predicted God would send a Savior. Jesus fulfills that prediction or prophecy.)**
- **Matthew 3:17 (Jesus is God's Son.)**
- **Matthew 6:8-15 (Jesus teaches us how to pray to God.)**
- **Matthew 8:26-27 (Jesus did many miracles and amazed many people.)**

- **Matthew 28:20b** (Jesus promises to be with us forever.)
- **John 3:16-17** (God loves us so much he sent Jesus to live and die for us. If we believe in Jesus, we'll live forever.)
- **John 14:6** (Jesus is the only way to be with God. Jesus is truth. Jesus is life.)
- **1 John 3:16** (Because of Jesus' example, we know how to love each other.)

When pairs are finished, have them each tell what they wrote on their handout. Congratulate the pairs on their investigative abilities.

Brilliant Deductions, Watsons

(You'll need a marker, tape, and either a whiteboard or newsprint taped to the wall. At the top write, "If we know...." In the middle write, "Then we know....")

Have students stay with their partners. Say: **Now that you've searched for clues, let's test your "private eye-Qs." For all the facts we learned, we'll come up with ideas about what they mean for us today.**

Call students' attention to the board.

Have pairs each read a fact (or facts) about Jesus they wrote on their "Clue Search" handout. After they read, have them each tape their handout under "If we know..." Then, as a large group, complete and write an example of "Then we know...." For example:

If we know... Jesus died for our sins because he loves us.
Then we know... love is what motivates him.

Continue until all the handouts are taped up and you've written an example of what each fact means. Then ask:

- **How is our private-eye search like our search to find meaning in life?**
- **Which of these "If...Then" statements best describes something that's already true about your life, and which describes something that's not yet true?**

- What's one conclusion that especially impacts you? Explain.
- Which conclusion seems most out-of-reach or difficult to live out for you?

You're Wanted

(You'll need white paper, markers, and tape.)

Say: **As you've deduced from your private-eye search, Jesus loves all of us, and he wants to be the center of our lives. Jesus wants *you*.**

Give students each a piece of white paper and some markers, and have them draw a small self-portrait in the middle of their piece of paper. Then have them stop and close their eyes, with their paper in front of them.

Say: **Be quiet right now—let's spend some time just listening to Jesus. That's all prayer really is—talking to Jesus and listening to Jesus. "Listening" really means paying attention to his "still, small voice." So, in just a moment, silently ask Jesus this simple question: "What do you really think of me?" After you ask, pause in the quiet and listen. You might get a word or a phrase or a Bible verse or even a picture in your head. Whatever it is, write it or draw it in the white space that's left on your paper. We'll do this for several minutes, so you might have a few things to add to your paper. First, I'll pray to lead us into this time: "Jesus, thank you for speaking to us. Help us hear your voice, just as you promised we could. We take authority over our own voice now, and we also tell your enemy to be quiet. We want to hear only your voice. Please, help us each hear what you really think of us...."**

Pause for three minutes in silence, giving students time to listen and add to their paper. Then have them each tape their paper around the "Wanted" poster.

6 Case Closed

(You'll need a marker. Copy and cut apart enough "Cross Patterns" on page 11 so each person has one. Gather five different-size sacks, and put the crosses in the smallest sack. Number the sacks from largest to smallest, and on each sack write one of Jesus' affirmations from below. Place the sacks inside each other—starting with the smallest and ending with the largest—so everything ends up in the largest sack.)

Write these affirmations from Jesus on the sacks:

- Bag 1—"Indeed, the very hairs of your head are all numbered. Don't be afraid; you are worth more than many sparrows" (Luke 12:7).
- Bag 2—"Do not be afraid, little flock, for your Father has been pleased to give you the kingdom" (Luke 12:32).
- Bag 3—"I give them eternal life, and they shall never perish; no one can snatch them out of my hand" (John 10:28).
- Bag 4—"Peace I leave with you; my peace I give you. I do not give to you as the world gives. Do not let your hearts be troubled and do not be afraid" (John 14:27).
- Bag 5—"You did not choose me, but I chose you and appointed you to go and bear fruit—fruit that will last. Then the Father will give you whatever you ask in my name" (John 15:16).

Form a circle, and show students the large sack (with the other sacks inside it). Pass around the sack while having students quietly sing the old children's song "Jesus Loves Me, This I Know." When the song ends, have the person holding the sack read aloud the affirmation on it. Then remove the outer sack and continue passing while students say the words again. Continue until all five affirmations are read. Have the person who opens the smallest sack present a cross to each person.

Encourage students to keep their cross on their bathroom mirror or in their school locker as a daily reminder of Jesus' love.

WANTED:

The identity of this man.

Those who help identify him will receive a
—REWARD—

CLUE SEARCH

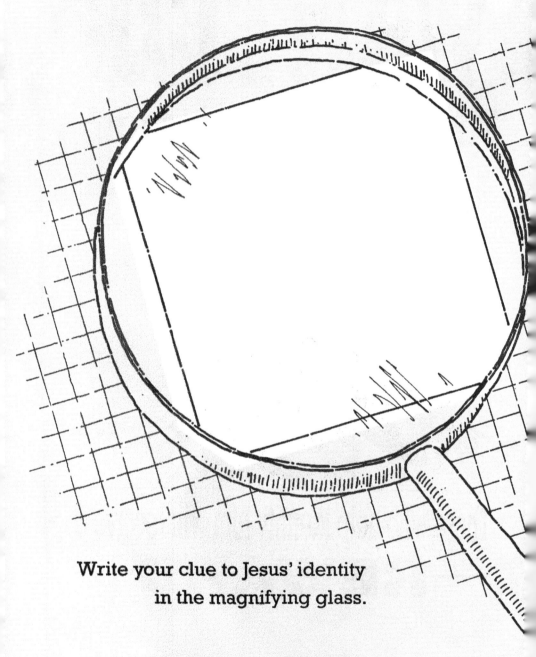

Write your clue to Jesus' identity
in the magnifying glass.

CROSS PATTERNS

Photocopy and cut apart these crosses.

the 13

most important

BIBLE LESSONS

for teenagers

WHO IS GOD?

By Paul Woods

Many young people view God the Father as a severe disciplinarian, concerned only about keeping people in line. Others see him as someone too great and far away to care about "insignificant" humans. Still others see him as merely an idea or unknowable "higher power."

But in the Bible, God reveals himself to us as a loving and perfect Father. Amid high divorce rates and abusive home situations, teenagers need a positive model of what a true father is—a father like God. He cares for us better than any earthly father ever could.

When students understand who their heavenly Father really is, they can begin to depend on God more and have a deeper relationship with him. Use this lesson to help students develop that understanding.

OBJECTIVES

In this lesson, students will:

- care for an egg to help them experience how God cares for us,
- brainstorm qualities of the perfect father,
- explore what the Bible says about who God is,
- experience what it's like to trust God to care for them, and
- determine ways they can depend on God more.

THE LESSON

Baby Eggbert

(You'll need an egg and a fine-line marker for each student. If you meet in a room where carpet or something might be damaged by raw eggs, you can boil the eggs first. However, this activity is more effective with raw ones.)

After students arrive, say: **Today we'll look at who God the Father really is. But first I'd like you to meet someone.**

Give each teenager an egg. Say: **Your egg is your child. Carefully draw a face on it, name it, and treat it the way a precious child should be treated. Hold it and keep it warm as much as possible, and obviously try to keep it from breaking.**

If you're using raw eggs, warn students of that at this point.

Allow a few minutes for egg preparation, and then move on to the next section. At five-minute intervals throughout the lesson's first three sections, ask teenagers how their "children" are doing and remind them of their responsibilities. If an egg breaks, replace it and debrief the loss of a "child" (see activity 4).

World's Greatest Father

(You'll need a marker and a whiteboard, or newsprint and tape. For each student you'll need an index card.)

Say: **Imagine we're a United Nations committee just formed to set up a World's Greatest Father contest. The first thing we need is a list of qualities each entrant must have. Let's form subcommittees of three to develop that list.**

Form groups of three, and have groups each create a list of at least seven qualities that will make someone eligible for this contest.

After five minutes, have someone from each group read aloud their list. Have someone write the unique qualities (ones not already listed by other groups) on the board as they're read.

From the qualities listed, have students work together to select the top 10 qualifications. Then ask:

- **Think about your answer to these next two questions, then write it on your card—we won't share our answers out loud. How does your earthly father stack up to these qualifications? If your dad was being graded on these qualifications, what grade would he get?**
- **What's easy or difficult for you about picturing God as your Father?**
- **For you, which quality from our list is most important in your relationship with God? Explain.**

Say: **God is a lot like the perfect human father. And the fatherhood concept can help us grow our relationship with God, who created us and cares for us.**

Remember to periodically remind students about their eggs. Encourage young people to lovingly care for their "children."

A Proper Introduction

(For each person, you'll need a pencil and a copy of the "Introducing... God!" handout on page 19.)

Distribute pencils and the "Introducing... God!" handouts, and have students follow the instructions. If they have limited Bible knowledge, have them work in groups of three to complete the handout.

When students finish, ask a few to read what they came up with. There are many good possibilities, but here's what someone might write:

Hi, I'm Ethan, and I'm here to introduce you to my father. He's generous and giving, and he really likes to give me good things. He likes when I obey him, and I enjoy being his child. I especially like him because he made me and takes care of me. I know he'll never treat me badly, and I know I can always count on him because he loves me. His love for me will last forever! I now present to you... God!

Once God is properly introduced to your group, ask:

- **What are some things God has given you and done for you?**
- **Think of a time when you doubted God's intentions or plan for you: Why is it sometimes difficult to believe that God is always good?**
- **What does our response to God say about our relationship with him?**

Say: **As our perfect heavenly Father, God wants what's best for us. And he wants us to be in relationship with him through our obedience, love, and service.**

Baby Eggbert Revisited

(No materials needed.)

Say: **You've been caring for your child for quite a while now. How's everyone doing?**

After students respond, ask:

- **Suppose your child did something you didn't like, such as rolling across the table away from you. What would you do in response?**
- **Some people think God is waiting to crush us when we do wrong. What would you say to someone who thought that way, and why?**
- **When we mess up, how do you think God reacts? How can we react, to restore our relationship with God?**

Eggbert and Me

(You'll need a Bible. For each person, you'll need a piece of paper and a pencil.)

Have someone read aloud 1 Peter 5:6-7. Say: **As the all-powerful Creator who loves us and cares about us so much, God our Father is completely trustworthy. Choose an area in your life where you need to depend on God's help more. It might be your future, school problems, relationships—anything. Then think about how you can begin depending on God more in that area.**

Give students each a piece of paper and a pencil, and have them write the area they've chosen and how they'll depend on God more.

When students have all written something down, ask them to form pairs. Have partners share with one another what they've written and how they plan to start trusting God more in that area. Have partners respond by encouraging one another with words such as, "God is trustworthy, and I know he'll help you when you depend on him."

6 All the King's Children

(For each person, you'll need a plastic egg and a fine-line marker.)

Gather all the egg "children" and then pass out plastic eggs to everyone. Have students each write their name on their plastic egg, fold their piece of paper from activity 5, and put it inside the plastic egg. Then have students stand in a circle, holding the plastic eggs.

Say: **People who believe in Jesus are all God's children—just as your eggs were your children today. God our Father takes perfect care of us and desires a deep relationship with us throughout our lives.**

Close by having kids look at their card from earlier in the lesson—the one with their "father grade" on it. Have them stare at that card as they ask Jesus how to pray for their dad. As they receive guidance on how to pray, give them silent time to do it. Then close by thanking God for loving us, and ask him to help young people follow through on trusting him more.

Encourage students to keep their plastic egg in a prominent place at home to remind them of God's love and care for them.

INTRODUCING...GOD!

Read each Bible passage to the right. Then fill in the missing words or phrases in the introduction. There are no right answers. Fill in anything you think fits based on the Scriptures you've read.

Jeremiah 31:3
Matthew 7:9-11
Acts 17:24-29
Ephesians 1:3-5

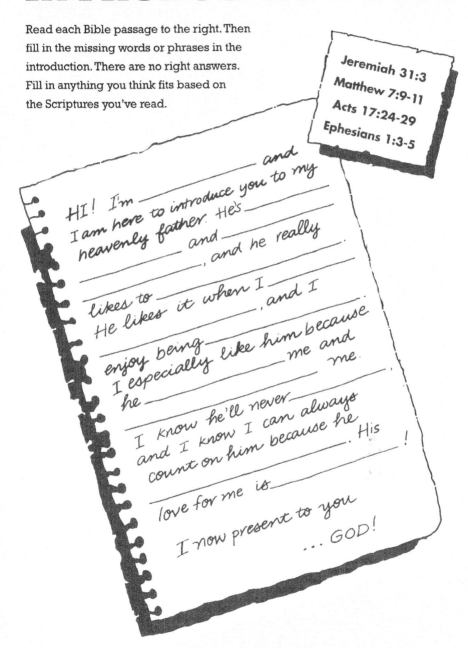

HI! I'm _____ and I am here to introduce you to my heavenly father. He's _____ and _____, and he really _____.

likes to _____. He likes it when I _____, and I enjoy being _____. I especially like him because he _____ me and me.

I know he'll never _____ and I know I can always count on him because he _____. His love for me is _____.

I now present to you ... GOD!

the 13

most important

BIBLE
LESSONS

for teenagers

WHO IS THE HOLY SPIRIT?

By Karen Dockrey

To teenagers, the Holy Spirit can seem like an invisible friend—something they can't see but like having around. But, of course, the Holy Spirit is no vaporlike ghostly thing—he's the third person in the Trinity, often referred to as "the Spirit of Jesus." The Holy Spirit knows the mind of Jesus, and helps us understand God by guiding us through our mind and heart, and by influencing our actions (John 16:13-15). What the Holy Spirit does in our lives is what makes him evident.

The Holy Spirit has many functions: fruit-producer, counselor, comforter, and convictor (John 14:15-17; John 16:7-11; and Galatians 5:22-23). The Holy Spirit is our on-site, personal guide to Jesus-centered living.

To handle tough situations and to live out their faith, students need the power that comes from the Holy Spirit. Use this lesson to help young people recognize the Holy Spirit's power and to show them how the Holy Spirit can impact their lives.

OBJECTIVES

In this lesson, students will:

- learn about the Holy Spirit as part of the Trinity,
- identify several of the Holy Spirit's functions,
- recognize that the Holy Spirit is for all Christians,
- play a game about the fruit of the Spirit, and
- discuss how the Holy Spirit's power is perfect and complete.

THE LESSON

Divine Trinity

(You'll need an ice cube, a glass of water, and a steaming cup of recently boiled water.)

Display the three forms of water. Ask:

- **What do ice, water, and steam have in common? How are they different?**
- **Which of these three would you say God is most like, and why?**

Say: **God is described in the Bible as the Trinity, which means three in one. Although we worship only one God, he functions in three ways: as the Father who created and cares for us, as the Son (Jesus) who died for us, and as the Holy Spirit, who we'll discuss today.**

Ask:

- **What is easy to understand about the concept of a "triune" God, and what is hard to understand about it?**

Job Description

(You'll need a copy of the "God Acts" handout on page 27, cut apart and placed inside a lunch-size paper sack. You'll also need to choose some background music and be ready to play it on a music player.)

Form a circle. Show the sack of "God Acts," and say: **This bag contains descriptions of God's actions. Let's find out which person of the Trinity does what. Remember that some actions are shared by the whole Trinity.**

Play music and have students pass the sack around the circle without looking inside. Stop the music at random intervals. Each time you stop the music, have the person holding the bag draw out one action and read it aloud.

Then brainstorm as a group which person of the Trinity does that action. Point out that distinguishing between actions isn't always possible because the three are really one God.

Function Unction

(You'll need a whiteboard, or newsprint and tape, a marker, and two Bibles.)

On the board, write the following description.

The Holy Spirit:

- lives within Christians to guide them,
- convicts Christians when they do wrong,
- guides Christians to do what is right,
- comforts Christians, and
- helps Christians understand God.

Don't let students see the board yet. Form two groups and give each group a Bible. Have groups each read aloud John 14:16-17 and John 16:5-15. Then have them locate in those Bible passages each function you listed. Have groups yell "Function!" whenever they find a function. Continue until students locate them all. When groups are finished, discuss the answers together.

Ask:

- At this point in your relationship with Jesus, which function of the Holy Spirit is most important to you, and why?
- How have you personally experienced the Holy Spirit functioning in you?

 ## Spirit Proof

(For every four people, you'll need a set of "Fruit Slap Cards" on pages 28 and 29, and a Bible.)

Read aloud Ephesians 1:13-14. Say: **When we believe in Jesus, the Holy Spirit comes to live within us. Then, as our relationship with Jesus grows, the Holy Spirit remains there to guide, comfort, counsel, and convict us.**

Ask:

- **What are some ways to identify an apple tree?**
- **What are some ways to identify a good friend?**
- **What are some ways to identify the Holy Spirit living within someone?**

Say: **The Holy Spirit produces fruit in a Christian's life, just as trees are known by their fruit and friends by their actions.**

To help students explore various aspects of the Holy Spirit's fruit, play Fruit Slap. Form groups of four or fewer, and have groups each sit in a circle. Give each group a shuffled deck of "Fruit Slap Cards" and a Bible. Have groups open their Bible to Galatians 5:22-23 and place the deck face down in the middle of the circle.

Have group members take turns turning over the top card in the deck. If the card reveals a fruit of the Spirit, students try to be the first to slap their hand on the card. The first person to slap the card keeps it. Students who slap a card that isn't a fruit of the Spirit must put one of their fruit cards back into the deck. If those students don't have any fruit cards yet, have them place the first card they win back in the deck.

After the game, have students each choose one fruit of the Spirit from Galatians 5:22-23 and describe how that fruit helps provide evidence of the Holy Spirit living in them. Ask:

- Why aren't these fruits always evident in the lives of people who follow Jesus?
- Can people show these fruits if they aren't Christians? Why or why not?

Say: The Holy Spirit lives in every Christian, but not all Christians let the Holy Spirit work. Christians choose daily whether to let the Holy Spirit produce fruit.

Power Provision

(For each person, you'll need a Bible.)

Say: The Holy Spirit's great power is available to everyone who wants it. The way to tap into the Holy Spirit's power is to believe in Jesus. Once you do that, God comes to live within you in the person of the Holy Spirit. You'll experience God's power as you let the Holy Spirit teach you about God and produce fruit such as love, joy, peace, patience, and faithfulness.

Have students each quietly read Galatians 5:22-23. Form a circle and say: **As a closing, say one fruit of the Spirit you see in the person on your right and how you see that fruit demonstrated. For example, "I see the fruit of peace in Manny's life because he stays calm and trusts God when things go wrong."**

After everyone has spoken, close with prayer by thanking God for sending the Holy Spirit to live in us.

the 13

most important

BIBLE
LESSONS

for teenagers

GOD ACTS

Photocopy and cup apart these strips, then fold and place each in a lunch-sized sack.

1. Created the earth

2. Came to live on earth as a human

3. Lives with Christians to guide them

4. Always was and always will be

5. Convicts Christians to do right

6. Convicts people of sin

7. Comforts Christians

8. Helps Christians know God

9. Died for our sins

10. Forgives Christians when they turn from their sin and ask forgiveness

11. All-knowing, all-present

FRUIT SLAP CARDS

SEXUAL IMMORALITY	**IMPURITY**	**DEBAUCHERY** (extreme self-indulgence)	**IDOLATRY** (worshipping something besides God)
WITCHCRAFT	**HATRED**	**DISCORD** (not getting along with others)	**JEALOUSY**
RAGE	**SELFISH AMBITION** (always trying to be #1)	**DISSENSION** (trying to split up a group of friends)	**FACTIONS** (people who dislike each other because of differing beliefs)

Copy and cut apart a set of these cards for every four people.
The words on the cards are from **Galatians 5:19-23.**

ENVY	DRUNKENNESS	ORGIES ("free sex" parties)	LOVE
JOY	PEACE	PATIENCE	KINDNESS
GOODNESS	FAITHFULNESS (loyalty)	GENTLENESS	SELF-CONTROL

the 13

most important

BIBLE
LESSONS

for teenagers

WHAT IS THE BIBLE?

By Scott C. Noon

"It's too hard to read."

"I'm busy, and it's too much information to sift through."

"It doesn't really make a difference in my everyday life."

Students can find lots of reasons not to read the Bible. But running through the excuses is one consistent thread: "The Bible intimidates me."

God never meant his Word to be intimidating. It's the most important way Jesus reveals himself to people who've made a faith commitment to him. Teenagers, especially, need the guidance the Bible offers— guidance for relationships, choices, and their purpose in life. But they'll never receive that guidance if they don't enjoy reading the book.

Through his Word, Jesus wants to relate to young people and show them how they can relate to him. Use this lesson to relieve teenagers' apprehension about the Bible and help them see how Jesus reveals himself through his Word.

OBJECTIVES

In this lesson, students will:

- explore what the Bible says about itself,
- discuss the Bible's overall theme,
- discover the importance of reading Scripture, and
- create a plan for daily Bible reading.

THE LESSON

Book Mixer

(For each person, you'll need a piece of tape and an index card with a famous book title written on it. Examples include War and Peace, The Adventures of Huckleberry Finn, The Grapes of Wrath, Animal Farm, To Kill a Mockingbird, Moby Dick, *and* A Tale of Two Cities. *It's okay to use a title more than once, but use as many different titles as possible.)*

On each person's back, tape one title card. Instruct students to walk around the room, asking yes-or-no questions about the identity of their books. They can ask no more than two questions of any one person, and answers can be only "yes" or "no."

After they discover the identity of their books, have students put their cards on the front of their shirts. Ask:

- **Why are these books so famous?**
- **When a book is "required reading," how does that affect your opinion about it?**

Say: **Today we'll look at the best-selling book of all time: the Bible. We'll discover why it has endured throughout the centuries and how it can have a huge impact on our lives today.**

Station Revelations

(For each person, you'll need a pencil and a copy of the "Station Revelations" handout on page 37. Set up five stations around the room, each with a Bible open to one of the passages listed below.)

Station 1—2 Timothy 3:16-17

Station 2—Hebrews 4:12

Station 3—Psalm 119:105

Station 4—James 1:22-24

Station 5—John 1:1-2, 14

Form five groups. A group can be one person. Number groups 1 through 5. Give students each a pencil and a "Station Revelations" handout.

Say: **Complete your handout by going to each of the five stations and reading the assigned Scriptures. The Bibles are already open to the passages.**

If any young people are unfamiliar with locating Bible passages, briefly explain the chapter-and-verse system.

Have students start at the station that corresponds to the number of their group. Then have them travel to the other stations to complete the handout.

When everyone has been to all the stations, review the handouts together. Ask a few kids to share what they discovered about the Bible. Then ask:

- **How is going from station to station like learning from the Bible in real life?**
- **How has the Bible impacted your own life?**
- **How has Jesus used the Bible to reveal something about himself to you?**

Bible Acts

(You'll need the "Bible Overview" on pages 38 and 39.)

Say: **The Bible is a collection of many different books. It contains two testaments, or "binding agreements between God and his people"— old and new. The Old Testament has 39 books, and the New Testament has 27, for a total of 66 books. But even though there are so many books, they all work together for one purpose: to show how God reveals himself to people. Let's act out some accounts from the Bible to get a better idea of how God reveals himself through his Word.**

Using the "Bible Overview," assign all the parts listed in the instructions. Have students act out their parts as you read the overview. For example, when you read "God created Adam and Eve," have "God" pretend to create "Adam" and "Eve."

Afterward, ask:

- **What's your reaction to this overview?**
- **What's important about this overview—and how everything ties together?**

Make a Covenant

(You'll need a sheet of paper. For each person, you'll need a pencil and a copy of the "Scripture-Reading Covenant" on page 40.)

Ask:

- **What type of "relationship" have you had with the Bible? When do you read it, and why?**

Share with young people your own thoughts about reading the Bible. To get started, answer these questions:

- **When did the Bible become important to you?**
- **What value do you place on daily Scripture reading?**
- **In what ways do you struggle with reading the Bible?**
- **When do you read?**

- What version do you read?
- How does the Bible guide you through problems and tough decisions?
- How does the Bible help you praise God?
- How do you apply what you read to your life?

Give students each a pencil and a "Scripture-Reading Covenant."

Say: **A covenant is like a contract. It can be an agreement between two people or between God and a person or group. In the Bible, a covenant was considered a serious binding agreement—broken only by the death of one of the parties.**

Allow time for young people to read through the covenant and make a plan for their own Bible-reading. (You can supplement this covenant with a specific reading plan, if desired.)

Have students form pairs and pray with their partners for Jesus to help them keep their new covenant. Encourage students to put their covenants in the front of their Bibles, and then periodically check in with them to see how they're doing.

Undercover Affirmations

(No supplies needed.)

Have students form a circle. Say: **We all know the adage "You can't judge a book by its cover." That's true of people, too. Share something positive about the person on your right that people might not see unless they looked beyond his or her "cover."**

Go around the circle, and have students each share about the person to the right.

6 **Thankful Closings**

(No supplies needed.)

Have students stay in the circle. Tell them to think of a sentence that expresses thanks to Jesus for something they've learned about the Bible. For example, someone might say, "Thanks for letting me see your love through the Bible" or "Thanks for giving me direction in life through your Word."

After everyone has spoken, close with a brief prayer thanking Jesus for the Bible and how it helps us grow closer to him.

STATION REVELATIONS

During the next few minutes, you'll have the chance to visit five stations, each displaying one of the Scriptures listed below. Each has something to say about the Bible and what it means for our lives. At each station, consider what the Scripture says about the Bible. Then follow the instructions below. After you've been to all five stations, return to your seat.

STATION #1

2 Timothy 3:16-17
God's Word has many uses in our lives. Write two ways God might use the Bible to impact your life.

STATION #2

Hebrews 4:12
Draw a picture that illustrates what this verse says to you.

STATION #3

Psalm 119:105
- How is the Bible a lamp to your feet?
- How is the Bible a light to your path?

STATION #4

James 1:22-24
- How is the Bible like a mirror?
- What does the Bible show you about yourself?

STATION #5

John 1:1-2, 14

Write a letter to Jesus, expressing your thoughts about him as God's greatest "message" to you.

_____
_____
_____
_____
_____
_____
_____

BIBLE OVERVIEW

Before you read this aloud, assign each of the following parts to a student. It's okay if someone has more than one part. But if you do ask someone to play two characters, assign parts that don't interact, such as Adam and Jesus, or Noah and Christians.

Characters: God, Adam, Eve, Noah, Abraham, Israel, the Promised Land, Jesus, apostles, Christians

Long ago, God created the world (pause to let God create the world). **Then he created Adam and Eve** (pause to let God create Adam and Eve), **but they rebelled against him** (pause to let Adam and Eve rebel against God) **and were banished from God's presence** (pause to let Adam and Eve hide from God).

As more and more people were born into the world, the world became more and more wicked. Finally, God decided to flood the earth and start over (pause to let God flood the earth). **But God saved one man—Noah—because he alone believed in God. Noah built an ark to carry him and his family through the storm** (pause to let Noah sail through the storm).

One of Noah's descendants—Abraham— became the father of a great nation, Israel (pause to let Abraham act like a father to Israel). **Eventually, God led Israel to a beautiful Promised Land, and it became Israel's home** (pause to let God lead Israel to the Promised Land).

In the centuries that followed, Israel went through many struggles and victories (pause to let Israel act this out). But even through its struggles, Israel hoped that one day God would send a Savior who'd bring peace forever (pause to let Israel hope in God).

When the time was right, God did send a Savior—his Son, Jesus (pause to let God send Jesus to Israel). Jesus was God in human form. He told people about God's love and peace (pause to let Jesus tell about God's love and peace). He also told people about their sin and their need for repentance (pause to let Jesus tell about people's sin and their need for repentance).

Although many people believed Jesus, most rejected him. They sentenced Jesus to die on a cross (pause to let Jesus die on a cross). Three days after his death, Jesus rose from the dead (pause to let Jesus rise from the dead). By doing this, Jesus broke down the wall between God and his people that resulted from Adam and Eve's sin (pause to let Jesus break down a wall). Then Jesus sent the apostles into all the world to share the message of Jesus' life and purpose with others (pause to let the apostles go into all the world). Jesus returned to heaven to be with God (pause to let Jesus return to God).

Jesus will return again to take all Christians with him to heaven (pause to let Jesus return to gather Christians to heaven). And all people who believe in Jesus as their Lord and Savior will be with God forever (pause to let everyone huddle around God).

THE END

Scripture-Reading Covenant

This covenant is between God and

_____.

Because my relationship with God is important to me and because
God desires to continue to teach and inspire me, I commit myself to the
following plan for Scripture reading:

GOALS I WANT TO REACH:

Example: I'll read the Bible for 20 minutes each day.
I'll read the entire Bible over the next year.

I'LL ...

MY PLAN FOR REACHING THESE GOALS:

Example: I'll set aside 20 minutes each day after school for reading the Bible.
I'll finish the Old Testament by September and read the New Testament in the fall.

I'LL ...

Signed: _____

Date: _____

IN THE BEGINNING

By Mike Gillespie

Teenagers often wonder how the earth, the universe, and humanity all fit together—and many worry about the environment's current and future condition. Young people are especially curious about their individual role in God's world, asking "Where do I belong?" and "How do I know if my life has any significance?"

God created our world—and each of us—for a unique purpose. He gave us the privilege and responsibility of being caretakers of creation. He also fashioned us to live in harmony with him, with other people, and with nature.

Use this lesson to help students explore their special place in God's creation and their role on the earth.

OBJECTIVES

In this lesson, students will:

- act out the creation account,
- compare the creation accounts,
- identify important themes in Genesis 1–2,
- experience being tied to creation, and
- celebrate God's gift of creation.

THE LESSON

➊ Clay Creations

(For each person, you'll need some modeling clay.)

Hand out modeling clay. Say: **Imagine God has just handed you this glob of formless material. Shape something from nature that you particularly enjoy.** After everyone is finished, have students each explain their creation. Ask:

- **What was fun or difficult about beginning with a formless mass?**
- **How did you decide what to create?**
- **In what ways is this activity similar to God creating the world?**

Say: **Sometimes we wonder how our world and all its beauty—and each of us!—got here. Let's explore Genesis 1–2 for some clues.**

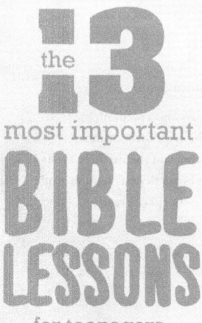

the **13** most important **BIBLE LESSONS** for teenagers

Start at the Beginning

(For each person, you'll need a Bible.)

Form six groups. A group can be one person. If you have fewer than six students, assign more than one Scripture passage to some people. Give students each a Bible, and assign them each one (or more) of these passages:

1. Genesis 1:3-5   4. Genesis 1:14-19

2. Genesis 1:6-8   5. Genesis 1:20-23

3. Genesis 1:9-13   6. Genesis 1:24-31

Say: **Each group has one day in God's creative process. I'm going to read the creation account from Genesis 1. As I read your group's passage, act out how you see that scene taking place. For example, the first group might huddle over someone and then have that person burst out of the huddle to represent the beginning of light. Be creative. You can use any objects in the room as props.**

Allow time for groups to decide how to act out their passage. Then read aloud Genesis 1, pausing after each section for the acting. Praise everyone's efforts. Then ask:

- What strikes you as most interesting or most perplexing about the creation process?
- What do you think the writer of Genesis 1 wanted to convey about God and our world?

Say: **Now let's keep reading. Genesis 2 tells the same account but in a different way.** Assign young people to read aloud different parts of Genesis 2:4-25. Then ask:

- What differences do you notice between these accounts?
- Why do you think they're both present in the Bible? What do they each tell you about God and his creation?

3 Branching Out

(For each person, you'll need a pencil and a copy of the "Creation Themes" handout on page 47.)

Say: **Let's explore the significance of these two accounts.**

Give students each a pencil and a "Creation Themes" handout. Form groups of three or fewer.

Say: **Read each Scripture on the handout, and write on the tree what you think is the most important point in that passage.**

Bring everyone together and discuss each passage. Here are possible themes:

- **Genesis 1:1—God is the creator.**
- **Genesis 1:4, 10, 12, 18, 21, 25, 31—God created all things good.**
- **Genesis 1:27—God created us in his image.**
- **Genesis 1:29-30—God made us caretakers of creation.**
- **Genesis 2:16-17—God gave us freedom with limits.**

Ask:

- **What does it practically mean that God created you in his image? that God created everything good?**
- **What's your reaction to being given freedom within limits? to being put in charge of God's creation?**

Say: **Although God created everything to be good, we haven't always been good stewards of what he made. Let's talk about this world that God made for us—and how we can better care for it.**

Globe Connections

(You'll need a picture or simply a rough drawing of the globe posted to a wall. For each person, you'll need a 6-foot piece of yarn, tape, an index card, and a pencil.)

Give students each a 6-foot piece of yarn and a piece of tape. Have them tie their yarn to their wrist and tape the other end of the yarn to the globe picture on the wall.

Give each person an index card, a pencil, and a piece of tape. Say: **We've damaged the earth in significant ways. God told us to take care of it, but we've abused that privilege. On your card, write one thing people have done to hurt the earth.**

As students finish, have them tape their cards to the globe (students should still be taped to the globe). When everyone's finished, have students take turns sharing what they wrote. Then ask:

- **How does it feel to be tied to an earth that is marred by what we've done to it?**
- **How have your deep ties to the earth impacted the way you treat it?**

Have students retrieve their cards from the globe. On the other side of the card, have them each write at least one thing they are already doing to keep the earth clean and good—as God intended. Ask them each to share one idea with the whole group.

5 Creation Celebration

(You'll need four large sheets of paper, tape, markers, and a Bible.)

Make and hang up signs that say "God," "Self," "Others," and "Nature." Form four groups, and have each group stand next to a different sign. Give each group a marker.

Say: **These four signs represent four areas in our lives God wants us to celebrate and enjoy. Look at your sign. Think about a specific way you can celebrate that area of your life. For example, someone in the "God" group might write, "I can worship God with my guitar." Someone in the "Others" group might write, "I can listen to a friend who's struggling, and offer to pray for him/her." Write your response on the sign, and then explain it to your group.**

When everyone's finished, gather in a circle and ask a few young people to repeat what they shared in their group. Then say: **God has given us many things to enjoy and take care of. As we close, let's praise God for the freedoms and responsibilities he's given.**

Read Psalm 8 responsively together as a closing prayer.

CREATION THEMES

Write the main points of each of
these Scriptures in the tree near
the appropriate Bible reference.

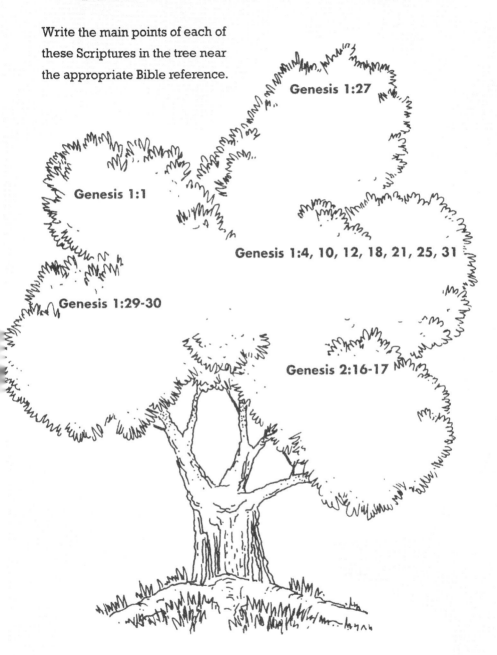

Genesis 1:27

Genesis 1:1

Genesis 1:4, 10, 12, 18, 21, 25, 31

Genesis 1:29-30

Genesis 2:16-17

the **13**

most important

BIBLE
LESSONS

for teenagers

THE HUMAN JOURNEY

By Ann Cannon

Life is a cycle: birth, development, growth, adolescence, young adulthood, adulthood, aging, and death.

But beyond the physical journey through life, we're also on a spiritual journey. For Christians, that journey begins and ends with Jesus. Through faith in him, we receive the promise of abundant life now and eternal life later.

Use this lesson to help students understand the nature of humanity in a fallen world—and to show them how Jesus' death and resurrection sets us free.

OBJECTIVES

In this lesson, kids will:

- consider their value as treasured children created in God's image,
- explore how sin severed our relationship with God,
- discover why we can't reach God on our own,
- understand God's gift of forgiveness through Jesus, and
- learn about God's promises for life today and for eternity.

THE LESSON

 Getting to Know Me

(For each person, you'll need paper, a marker, scissors, and a safety pin. Copy and cut apart the "Footprint Steps" on pages 55 through 57. Tape the footprints in numerical order to the walls of your meeting room.)

As young people arrive, have them each make a name tag, following the instructions on Footprint #1. Encourage students to ask one another for positive, descriptive words about themselves, pin their name tags to their clothing, and then read one another's name tags.

After a few minutes, call everyone together. Say: **Life is a journey with many physical changes, but each person also experiences a spiritual journey. Today we'll travel to see what's involved in the spiritual side of being human.**

Have someone read aloud Footprint #2. Have students each respond.

Say: **Your feelings about your lives—even the way you feel about yourself—can change from day to day. But Jesus always sees the truth about who you are.**

 The Good News

(You'll need a large mirror with a "You are made in God's image" sign attached to the front. Turn the mirror toward the wall. For each person, you'll need a copy of the "Made in God's Image" handout on page 58, a Bible, and a pencil.)

Read aloud the instructions on Footprint #3, and ask someone to do what it says. Have students each look at their image in the mirror. Then ask:

- **To you, what does it mean to be made in God's image?**
- **What's comforting about that? What's intimidating about that?**

Say: **Let's look at characteristics that make people and God similar.**

Give students each a "Made in God's Image" handout, a Bible, and a pencil. Designate each corner of the room as a different letter: A, B, C, or D. Designate the center of the room as E. Read aloud the first Scripture, and allow 10 seconds for students to decide which answer from the list on the right is correct. Then have them run to the part of the room that corresponds to their answer. After everyone chooses an answer, give the correct answer. Repeat the procedure for the next Scripture.

When everyone's finished, review the answers and discuss students' responses. The correct answers are 1. D, 2. C, 3. E, 4. B, 5. A.

Afterward, say: **You're important to God, who made you to be like him.**

Proceed to Footprint #4, asking students to respond to each question.

The Bad News

(You'll need Bibles, several newspapers, a large garbage bag, a trash can or bucket, and eight inflated balloons, each with one of the "Missing the Mark" Scriptures from page 59 inside. Use a marker to write "Psalm 53:1-3" on a newspaper.)

Say: **Although you're very different from the people around you, all humans share something in common.**

Hold up the newspaper with Psalm 53:1-3 written on it. Ask someone to read aloud Psalm 53:1-3 from a Bible as the others listen for what the verses say about the condition of people. Ask:

- **What's your reaction to these verses—especially considering the fact that you're made in God's image?**
- **What prevents people from having a relationship with God?**

Read aloud Footprint #5, and do what it says. Give each team several newspapers. Tell teams they have three minutes to find the most examples of sin and corruption in the newspapers. Instruct students to tear out headlines, pictures, stories, advertising, and other items related to sin.

After three minutes, call on each team to share its "sins." Say: **Now we need to clean up our mess. Pass around the garbage bag. Have students wad up all the newspapers as quickly as possible.**

Then say: **Look how dirty your hands are! After identifying all those sins in the newspapers, we're covered in guilt and the consequences of all those sins.**

Don't allow students to wash their hands. Read aloud Footprint #6, letting young people brainstorm responses to the questions.

Go to Footprint #7 and say: **Sin is like an arrow that misses the mark.** Read aloud Footprint #7.

Have someone read aloud Romans 3:23. Have students brainstorm a definition for sin.

Illustrate Romans 3:23 by having students attempt to shoot a balloon into a trash can or bucket. Set the "firing line" about 5 feet away. After everyone has had a turn, ask:

- **How is missing the trash can like being human?**

For ideas on how to hit the target, have students pop the balloons and look up the Bible verses inside. After students have read their passages, ask:

- **What do these verses say about "missing the mark"?**

Read aloud Footprint #8, allowing students to respond to each question.

The Best News

(You'll need a damp towel, a wadded-up sheet of newspaper, and a bowl of dirt. For each person, you'll need a flimsy paper plate, two pieces of yarn, and a marker.)

Say: **No one can overcome sin by acting religious or by living a strict life.**

Ask someone to read aloud Footprint #9. Say: **God loves you enough to create a way back into fellowship with him. That comes through Jesus Christ.**

Read aloud John 3:16. Say: **God has made a way for you, but you have a choice. I'll set three items on the table. You'll each have a chance to choose an item for washing away your inky guilt and sins. But first, let's look more closely at the sin in our lives.**

Give students each a flimsy paper plate, two pieces of yarn, and a marker. Say: **On your plate, write a sin you recognize in your life. No one will see this. Punch holes in opposite sides of your plate, tie strings in the holes, and tie the plate onto your face with the sin facing toward your face.** Be sure students can't see around their "masks."

Set out the damp towel, the wadded-up newspaper, and a bowl of dirt. Number the items (students won't know which number refers to which item). Then have students come to the table one at a time and say by number which item they want to try to wash off the ink. Tell everyone to be silent during this activity.

After everyone has had a turn, have students each remove their mask and see the results. Ask:

- **Why was it hard to make a good choice?**
- **How are your masks like sin in your life?**

Say: **To come to Jesus, you must be willing to put sin away. You did that by removing your mask. Jesus removes your mask when you ask for his forgiveness.**

Let students wipe their hands with the damp towel as you read aloud 1 John 1:9.

Read aloud Footprint #10, allowing students to respond to each question.

Who, Me?

(For each person, you'll need a Bible, a pencil, a sheet of paper, and a piece of tape.)

Say: **Not only does Jesus remove the guilt of sin from our lives, he also promises to help us be more like him.**

Read aloud Matthew 5:3-12. Have someone read aloud Footprint #11, and have students follow the instructions. Hand out pencils, and allow time for students to write on the back of their name tag. Call on a few young people to share their new name tags. Encourage everyone to place the name tags in a place where they can see the promises daily.

Read aloud Footprint #12. Ask:

- **How has this lesson changed your perspective on your relationship with Jesus?**

Give students each a sheet of paper and a piece of tape. Have them tape their papers to their name tags. Say: **For our closing, let's recognize how God has helped each of us become more like him. On each person's sheet, write one way you see Jesus' character in him or her.**

When everyone is finished, let students read their name tags. Then close with prayer, thanking God for helping us become more like him each day.

FOOTPRINT STEPS 1-4

Copy and cut apart these footprints, and tape them to your meeting-room walls.

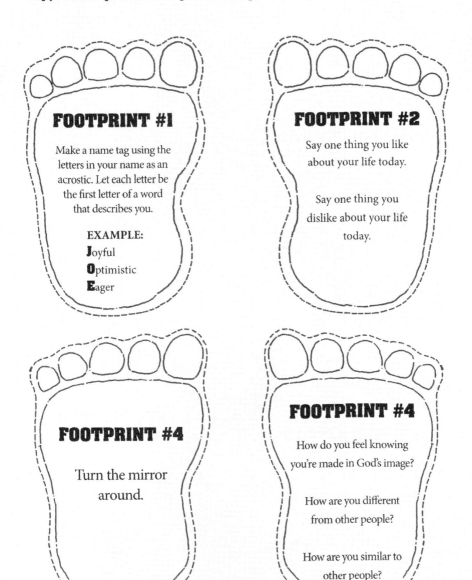

FOOTPRINT #1

Make a name tag using the letters in your name as an acrostic. Let each letter be the first letter of a word that describes you.

EXAMPLE:
Joyful
Optimistic
Eager

FOOTPRINT #2

Say one thing you like about your life today.

Say one thing you dislike about your life today.

FOOTPRINT #4

Turn the mirror around.

FOOTPRINT #4

How do you feel knowing you're made in God's image?

How are you different from other people?

How are you similar to other people?

FOOTPRINT STEPS 5-8

Copy and cut apart these footprints, and tape them to your meeting-room walls.

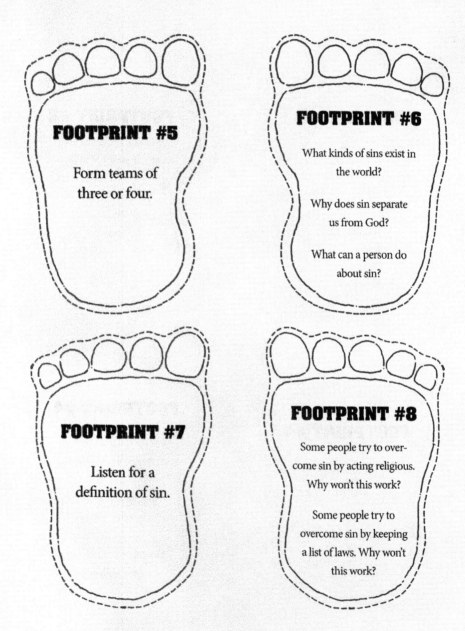

FOOTPRINT #5

Form teams of three or four.

FOOTPRINT #6

What kinds of sins exist in the world?

Why does sin separate us from God?

What can a person do about sin?

FOOTPRINT #7

Listen for a definition of sin.

FOOTPRINT #8

Some people try to overcome sin by acting religious. Why won't this work?

Some people try to overcome sin by keeping a list of laws. Why won't this work?

FOOTPRINT STEPS 9-12

Copy and cut apart these footprints, and tape them to your meeting-room walls.

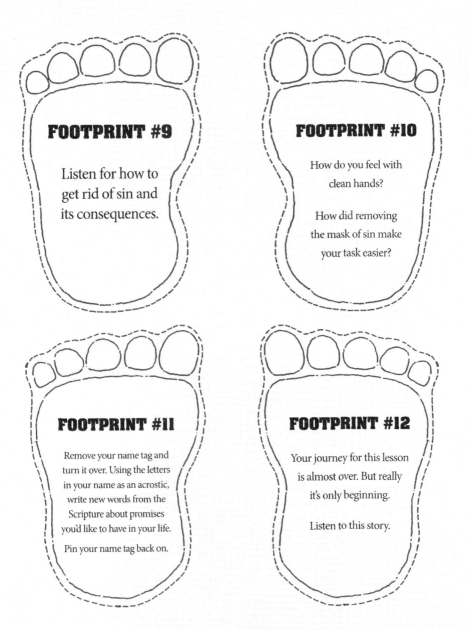

FOOTPRINT #9

Listen for how to get rid of sin and its consequences.

FOOTPRINT #10

How do you feel with clean hands?

How did removing the mask of sin make your task easier?

FOOTPRINT #11

Remove your name tag and turn it over. Using the letters in your name as an acrostic, write new words from the Scripture about promises you'd like to have in your life.

Pin your name tag back on.

FOOTPRINT #12

Your journey for this lesson is almost over. But really it's only beginning.

Listen to this story.

MADE IN GOD'S IMAGE

Match each Scripture to the characteristic that describes how humans are made in God's image.

1. Genesis 1:26

a. compassionate, kind, humble, gentle, patient, forgiving, loving

2. Psalm 8:4-5

b. all equal in God's sight

3. Psalm 119:73

c. crowned with majesty and glory

4. Galatians 3:28

d. power over all living things in God's world

5. Colossians 3:10, 12-14

e. understanding; the ability to reason

COMPASSIONATE

power over all things

LOVING

KIND

PATIENT

FORGIVING

ability to reason

ALL EQUAL

HUMBLE

crowned with majesty

crowned with glory

MISSING THE MARK

Copy and cut apart these verses, and then place each in a separate balloon.

Psalm 51:3-4	Romans 7:19
Mark 14:38	Romans 7:22-23
Romans 7:15	Romans 7:25
Romans 7:18	1 John 1:8-9

the **13**

most important

BIBLE
LESSONS

for teenagers

WHY DOES LIFE HURT?

By Arlo Reichter

Life isn't fair. We all face tough times. A teenager who loves Jesus gets killed by another teenager who's driving drunk—he survives without a scratch. "If God loves me, why does he let all these bad things happen?" The Bible explores God's perspective on sin, evil, and suffering—and why they exist in the world.

Use this lesson to help students understand why life hurts—and how Jesus brings healing.

OBJECTIVES

In this lesson, students will:

- consider the good and bad things that happen to people;
- explore how people in the Bible responded to sin, evil, and suffering;
- learn why it's better to live Jesus' way; and
- affirm one another for trusting Jesus—even during hard times.

THE LESSON

Ordering Events

(You'll need paper, pencils, markers, and a whiteboard, or newsprint and tape.)

Form two groups, and give each a sheet of paper and a pencil. Have one group list 10 bad things that've happened in the last month. Have the other group list 10 good things that've happened in the last month. Allow three minutes for groups to make their lists.

Call time, and have groups each rank their lists from 1 to 10 (1 = worst or best; 10 = "least worst" or "least best"). Then have groups write their lists in order so everyone can see them. Have a representative from each group explain the list, telling why they ranked the events that way.

Say: **Life isn't fair. Bad things happen to good people; good things happen to bad people. Why does evil exist in a world that God created as good? Let's explore the Bible's answers about sin, evil, and suffering.**

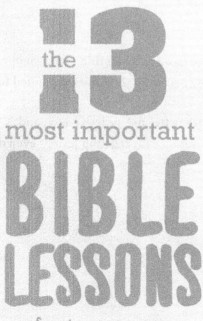

"Job" Descriptions

(For each person, you'll need a Bible and a copy of the "Glance at Job" handout on page 66.)

Give each person a Bible and a "Glance at Job" handout. Read aloud the opening statement on the handout. Form groups of four. Have groups each review the Scriptures listed on the handout and develop a brief skit that illustrates the four major acts.

When groups are ready, have them present their skits. Praise each group's efforts, and comment on how each skit parallels Job's story.

After all groups have presented their skits, ask:

- How did you feel as you acted out Job's story?
- In what ways is Job's story like your own?
- Why did God allow bad things to happen to Job?
- Why does God sometimes allow bad things to happen to us?

Say: **Like Job, we need to listen to God, recognize his justice, repent of our sins, and accept God as Creator, sustainer, and guide of our lives.**

Headline News

(You'll need a whiteboard or newsprint and tape, five markers, and five Bibles.)

Read aloud Matthew 5:45b. Say: **Good and bad things happen to everyone. But life with Jesus promises certain good things that can't come any other way. Jesus takes ugly things and makes them beautiful. And a life without Jesus means certain bad things are inevitable.**

Form five groups. A group can be one person. Draw a line down the middle of the board. On one side, write "Life With Jesus." On the other side, write "Life Without Jesus." Give each group a marker and a Bible. Assign each group one of these Bible passages:

- **Ephesians 2:1-10**
- **Ephesians 4:17-32**
- **Ephesians 5:1-20**
- **Colossians 2:6-17**
- **Colossians 3:5-17**

Have groups each read their Bible passage and then pull examples from the Scripture of "Life With Jesus" or "Life Without Jesus" and write them under the appropriate heading. For example, under "Life With Jesus," students might write "made alive in Christ." Under "Life Without Jesus," students might write "dead in sin."

When groups are finished, have them take turns explaining what they wrote and how it impacts their lives. Ask:

- **What are some things you gain by living your life with Jesus?**
- **What are the consequences for living outside a relationship with Jesus?**
- **Why doesn't Jesus always keep bad things from happening to Christians?**

Say: **It's true that bad things happen to good people. But Jesus gives us the resources—his love, fellowship with other Christians, and truths from God's Word—to help us deal with life's experiences. These resources are available to us when we choose to live in relationship with Jesus.**

Cloud Cheers

(You'll need a Bible. For each person, you'll need a pencil and a piece of tape.)

Say: **Job never really discovered God's reasons for allowing bad things to happen to him. In the same way, some bad things that happen to us will never be explained until we get to heaven. But many Christians have gone before us, leaving an example to persevere even when we don't know all the answers.**

Read aloud Hebrews 12:1-2. Give everyone a pencil and a piece of tape, and have students draw a cloud on the back of one of their handouts. Have students each tape their cloud to their back. Inside each person's cloud, have students list how that person helps them trust God, even in hard times. When students are finished, let them read their clouds.

Close with the following prayer. Have students repeat each line after you.

Thank you, God, for my cloud of witnesses.

Help me move away from sin.

Keep me running toward the goal you've set for me.

And allow us to support one another along the way. Amen.

GLANCE AT JOB

Job's story in the Old Testament provides a classic example of bad things happening to good people. Job's friends believed God always rewards good and punishes bad, so when bad things happened to Job and his family, his friends assumed Job had sinned. Although sin hadn't caused his suffering, Job did become arrogant amid suffering and evil. He eventually recognized his sin and repented.

In your group, create a contemporary play containing four major acts similar to the four acts of Job. You can use any characters, time in history, or settings you want. But your skit must illustrate the points made in Job's life. The four major acts in his story are:

1. Job's Arrogance (Job 29:1-25)

2. Job Listens to God (Job 33:1-14)

3. God Is Just (Job 36:22-26)

4. Job Repents (Job 42:1-6)

FAMILY OF FAITH

By Karen Dockrey

A faith commitment is more than a one-time, fire-insurance experience. It's a transformation, a lifestyle, a family adoption. When we believe in Jesus, we join other Christian brothers and sisters as a family of faith. As in all families, we'll experience joy and heartache, confusion and reaffirmation, growth and regression. Most importantly, we share the security of always belonging to Jesus, always being loved by Jesus, and always being understood by Jesus. These assurances give Christians the foundation for growth and maturity.

Faith is a journey—a process. It begins with trusting Jesus as Savior and Lord and continues through life on earth. This lesson addresses Christian faith in three stages, which are closely related and not always easy to delineate:

- placing faith in Jesus,
- increasing in Christlikeness, and
- enjoying Jesus in heaven.

Use this lesson to help students understand their faith as a growing relationship with Jesus that culminates in heaven.

OBJECTIVES

In this lesson, students will:

- notice how and why Christians are different,
- distinguish between joy based on circumstances and joy based on a relationship with Jesus,
- see faith from Jesus' perspective,
- create images of heaven, and affirm their need for faith in Jesus.

THE LESSON

A Christian I Know

(You'll need a ball of yarn.)

Have students form a circle. Hold up a ball of yarn, and explain that everyone will tell about a person they'd consider a mature Christian, and what that person's life is like. You start. After you talk about a mature Christian, toss the yarn to someone else, but hold on to the end so a string stretches between you and that person. Have that person share next, then have him or her hold onto the end of the yarn and toss the ball to a third person. Continue until everyone has held the yarn and a web of yarn is created in the circle.

Ask:

- **What are some distinguishing characteristics of Christians?**
- **What do all those people have in common?**

Say: **The beginning of Christian faith is as simple as trusting Jesus as Savior and Lord. Living out faith can be as intriguing and as complex as the yarn web we've created. Today we'll discover some of these complexities, mysteries, and joys.**

A New Life

(For each person, you'll need a piece of yarn and a Bible.)

Cut foot-long strips of yarn from the web, and give one to each person. Say: **On the floor, "draw" with your piece of yarn something that represents joy.**

When students are finished, have them explain their shapes. Note that some shapes emphasize joy from an event, while others emphasize joy from relationships. Discuss the difference between happiness based on circumstances and happiness based on a relationship with Jesus.

Say: **Faith in Jesus brings the deepest and longest-lasting joy possible. That joy persists no matter the circumstances. It provides a sense of well-being and the assurance that no matter what happens, Jesus is with us and will take care of us.**

Say: **During this lesson, we'll focus on one Bible book to learn three basic truths about a faith commitment. The theme of Philippians is joy in Christ.**

If needed, show students where to find Philippians in their Bibles. Then say: **The three truths we'll study spell BIG:**

- **Begin trusting Jesus,**
- **Increase in Christlikeness, and**
- **Go to heaven.**

Say: **At some point, we begin our faith relationship with Jesus. Then while we live on earth, we increase in Christlikeness. After we die, we go to heaven, where we live forever in the presence of Jesus and others who've trusted in him.**

Trading Steps

(You'll need a Bible, a whiteboard or newsprint and tape, and a marker.)

Ask:

- **When does a relationship with God start in a person's life?**

Read aloud Philippians 1:6. On the board, write the words "need," "love," "believe," and "relationship." Circle the words as you mention them. Say: **Our journey with God begins by understanding our need for Jesus. Only he can meet our need for belonging and intimacy. Then you recognize that Jesus loves you even though you don't deserve it. Finally, we believe in Jesus and his love. A faith commitment is a relationship rather than a set of rules or a religion. Like any love relationship, a faith commitment grows and deepens as you learn more about how to follow and serve Jesus.**

Now write these words and phrases: "good deeds," "religiousness," and "acknowledging God's existence." Ask:

- **Why don't these things make someone a Christian or accurately represent a faith commitment?**
- **What misunderstandings have you heard people express about faith?**

A New View

(You'll need a Bible. For each person, you'll need a piece of blue- or rose-colored plastic wrap, a copy of the "Eyes of Christ" handout on page 75, and scissors.)

Give students each a piece of blue- or rose-colored plastic wrap, and have them look through it. Ask:

- **How does the world look different now?**
- **What do you see that you wouldn't see without these "glasses"?**

Say: A faith relationship is a process of becoming more and more like Jesus Christ. Part of this process is seeing yourself, your relationships, and the world in a different light.

Read aloud Philippians 2:1-18. Give students each an "Eyes of Christ" handout and scissors. Have students make their glasses and put them on.

Ask:

- How does seeing through Jesus' eyes affect your actions? your relationships? your faith?
- How do you see circumstances differently because you're a follower of Jesus?

Rolling Applications

(You'll need a Bible. You'll also need a copy of the "Philippians Cube" on page 76 and a copy of the "Experience Cube" on page 77. Assemble the cubes beforehand.)

Say: Living your faith is a step-by-step, day-to-day process. It means looking at things the way Jesus sees them and responding the way Jesus would respond.

Invite someone to read aloud Philippians 3:10-16. Hold up the "Philippians Cube" and point out the six phrases from Philippians 3:10-14 on the sides. Hold up the "Experience Cube" and explain these are experiences we face daily. Say: Take turns rolling both cubes and naming a way to live your faith. For example, if you roll "to know Christ" and "how I spend my free time," you might say, "I'll choose music that encourages me to understand and live like Jesus rather than music that confuses or contradicts my relationship with Jesus."

After everyone has had a turn, ask:

- How does living like Jesus bring joy?
- How does obeying Jesus bring freedom?

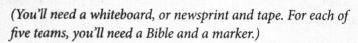

6 Forever Results

(You'll need a whiteboard, or newsprint and tape. For each of five teams, you'll need a Bible and a marker.)

Say: **Christians on earth are far from perfect, and conditions here are far from perfect. But there's a place with perfect conditions and perfect people. That place is heaven, and if you believe in Jesus as your Savior, you'll spend eternity with him there.**

Read aloud Philippians 3:20-21. Explain that heaven is our home—our final destination—and when we die or when Jesus returns to earth, we'll go there to be with him.

Ask:

- **How does knowing about heaven affect how you feel about life on earth?**
- **How does it affect your desire to have a relationship with Jesus now?**

Say: **Describing heaven is difficult because it's so different from anything we've ever experienced. It's like describing color to a blind person or adulthood to an infant. Philippians tells us briefly about heaven, but Revelation 21 provides images of heaven that help us understand what it will be like.**

Form five teams, and give each team a Bible and a marker. A team can be one person. Assign each team one of the following passages:

- **Revelation 21:1-4**
- **Revelation 21:5-7**
- **Revelation 21:9-14**
- **Revelation 21:15-21**
- **Revelation 21:22-27**

Have teams each draw on the board a picture that represents their Bible passage. Comment on each team's drawing, and point out how it expresses Scripture. Ask:

- **Which image of heaven is your favorite, and why?**
- **How does this image connect to your life now?**

Read aloud Revelation 21:8. Say: **Not everyone goes to heaven. Some people go to hell because they choose to reject Jesus and a relationship with him.** Ask:

- Why might people choose to stay separated from Jesus?
- How does hell begin the moment someone rejects Jesus?
- How does heaven begin the moment someone puts his or her faith in Jesus?

Freed From and To

(You'll need a whiteboard, or newsprint and tape, as well as several markers.)

Ask:

- To you, what's the appeal of living for Jesus?
- What freedom does Jesus offer us that we can't find in the world?

On the board, write these headings: "Freed From..." and "Freed To...." Provide markers for students to write pairs of answers. Possibilities include:

Freed From...

- loneliness
- confusion
- powerlessness
- meaninglessness
- many problems

Freed To...

- belong to Jesus and his family
- have Jesus help me understand
- receive Jesus' power
- have a purpose
- follow Jesus in how I live

Ask:

- Which is your favorite "Freed From ... Freed To" completion, and why?
- How can you respond to the freedom that Jesus offers?

8 Why Jesus

(You'll need a Bible. For each person, you'll need an index card and a pencil.)

Ask:

- **What's so important about trusting in Jesus?**

Say: **Without Jesus, we're incomplete. As a philosopher said, each of us has a God-shaped emptiness, and only Jesus can fill it.**

Read aloud the promises in Philippians 4:13 and 4:19. Give everyone an index card and a pencil. Have students write responses to these questions:

- **What comes to mind when you hear each of these promises?**
- **How might they impact the way you live out your faith in Jesus?**

Have students form a circle. Invite them to talk with Jesus about their relationship with him. Suggest they start their prayers with "Jesus, I'm glad you..." or "I want to show I love you by...."

Close by reading aloud Philippians 4:13 and 4:19 again.

EYES OF CHRIST

Cut apart these glasses, fold as marked, and hold them to your eyes.

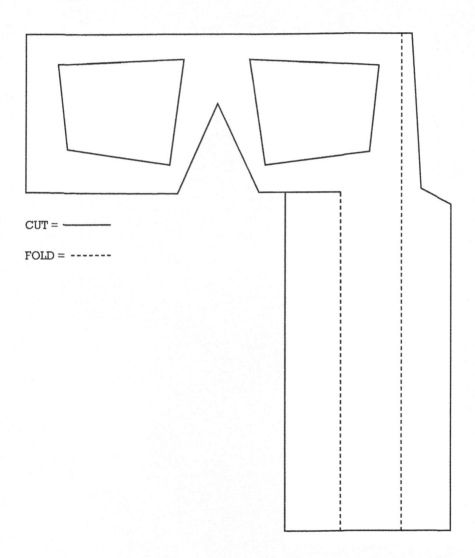

CUT = ———

FOLD = - - - - - - -

PHILIPPIANS CUBE

Copy, cut apart, and assemble this cube.

fold under

PHILIPPIANS CUBE

PHILIPPIANS CUBE

fold under

Let us live up to what we have already attained.

PHILIPPIANS CUBE

PHILIPPIANS CUBE

fold under

PHILIPPIANS CUBE

PHILIPPIANS CUBE

Forgetting what is behind and straining toward what is ahead.

PHILIPPIANS CUBE

PHILIPPIANS CUBE

PHILIPPIANS CUBE

PHILIPPIANS CUBE

PHILIPPIANS CUBE

To know Christ.

PHILIPPIANS CUBE

PHILIPPIANS CUBE

PHILIPPIANS CUBE

PHILIPPIANS CUBE

PHILIPPIANS CUBE

Press on toward the goal to win the prize for which God has called me.

PHILIPPIANS CUBE

PHILIPPIANS CUBE

fold under

fold under

fold under

PHILIPPIANS CUBE

PHILIPPIANS CUBE

Becoming like him in his death, and so some-how, to attain to the resurrection from the dead.

PHILIPPIANS CUBE

PHILIPPIANS CUBE

PHILIPPIANS CUBE

PHILIPPIANS CUBE

I press on to take hold of that for which Christ Jesus took hold of me.

PHILIPPIANS CUBE

PHILIPPIANS CUBE

EXPERIENCE CUBE

Copy, cut apart, and assemble this cube.

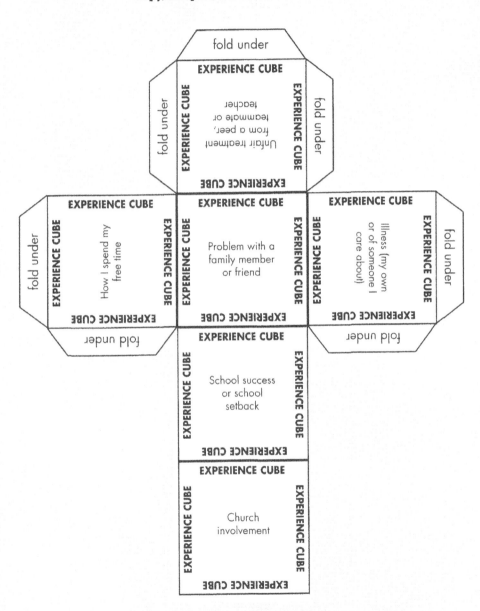

the 13

most important

BIBLE
LESSONS

for teenagers

WHY THE CHURCH?

By Paul Woods

"Why should I go to church? It's just a bunch of old people who frown at me because of my hair!"

"I just don't fit in there. And I'm sick of boring sermons."

"I have one day of the week to sleep in, so give me a break!"

Teenagers don't always have positive thoughts about church. So it's important to show them what church offers:

- a place where they can learn about Jesus and grow in faith,
- a place where they can serve Jesus as part of his body, and
- a place of belonging where they can interact with other followers of Jesus.

Young people desperately need all those things. Use this lesson to help students see what the church can really mean to them.

OBJECTIVES

In this lesson, students will:

- sort out truths and misconceptions about the church,
- examine what the Bible says about the church,
- experience working together, with each person contributing,
- demonstrate how Christians need one another, and
- celebrate being part of the church.

THE LESSON

What's the Church Anyway?

(For each group of three or four, you'll need tape and a copy of the "Is It or Isn't It?" handout on page 84. Cut apart the phrases, making a set for each group. On a whiteboard or newsprint, write these two headings: "The Church Is..." and "The Church Isn't....")

Form groups of three or four. Say: Today we'll look at the church. First let's have some fun with what we know about it. I'll give each group a set of phrases that complete one of these headings: "The Church Is ..." or "The Church Isn't...."

When I say "go," decide where the phrases fit. Then tape them under the proper heading. If you're right, you win. If not, take them back to your group and try again.

Give each group tape and a set of phrases from the "Is It or Isn't It?" handout. Then start the game.

The way the phrases are listed on the handout is correct. When a group gets them all correct, declare the winner. Then review each phrase, discussing why it does or doesn't describe the church.

Why Church?

2 *(You'll need Bibles, pencils, and paper.)*

If you have fewer than 12 students, do this activity as a single group, having the group work with all three Scripture passages. If you have more students, form three groups and assign one passage to each group:

- Matthew 28:18-20
- Acts 2:42-47
- Ephesians 4:11-16

Form a circle. Give groups each a sheet of paper and a pencil. Say: **Imagine your group is a college creative-writing class. The professor has assigned you a Scripture passage to read and asked you to write a brief essay discussing the church, based on that Scripture.**

Your essay must be as many sentences long as there are people in your group, and each person needs to write one sentence. You can discuss what to cover and help one another decide what to write. **Begin with the person with the most red on.**

Have students read aloud as they write. When everyone's finished, have groups take turns reading their essays aloud. Ask:

- **What did you learn about the church from these Bible passages?**
- **From these Bible passages, why would you say Jesus established the church?**
- **How was writing the essay together like serving Jesus in the church?**
- **In your own words, what does it mean to be part of "the body of Christ"?**

3 What's It to Me?

(You'll need an old paperback book at least ¾-inch thick that can be torn up.)

Say: **We've talked about what the church is and why Jesus started it, but now let's look at what that means to us.**

Pass around the book, and challenge students to tear it in half while keeping it shut tight. Allow five seconds for each attempt.

When everyone has tried and failed, open the book and tear it apart, giving students each a 20- to 30-page section. Have students each tear their section in half. Ask:

- **In what ways is this book like the church?**
- **How are the book's small sections like individual Christians?**

Say: **In the church, we can pull together and prevent any of us from being torn apart. Christians truly are family members on the same side—available to help and support one another.**

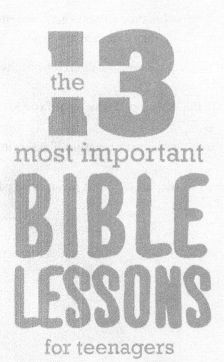

the 13 most important BIBLE LESSONS for teenagers

❹ A Place for Me?

(You'll need index cards and pencils.)

Pass out a card and pencil to everyone. Say: **Let's consider how we can take a more active part in the church, by giving and receiving.**

Say: **On one side of your card, write one way you can be a support to someone else in the church. On the other side, write one way you can lean on other people in the church more for help.**

When students are finished, have them form pairs. Have students share with their partner what they wrote on their card. Then have students tell their partner one reason they're glad he or she is part of the church. Encourage students to be sincere and serious with their encouragement.

Read aloud 1 Corinthians 12:12-27. Say: **In the church, God has given us a place to belong and be needed, a place to learn about him, and a place to serve him. And, as Jesus said in Matthew 28:20, he'll be with us always!**

Close with a prayer thanking God for the church.

IS IT OR ISN'T IT?

Copy and cut apart the following phrases, without the headings.

The Church Is . . .

people who make a lot of mistakes while trying to serve God.

a place for hurting people to find comfort and help.

something set up by God to help his people through life.

a group of people sharing common faith and hope in Jesus Christ.

a group of people gifted by God to serve him together.

The Church Isn't . . .

a place for old people to gather and listen to a dull sermon.

a place for good people to meet together and be happy about their goodness.

an old building with stained-glass windows.

a bunch of cranky people who want to keep teenagers from having a good time.

the place where God lives.

PRAYER POWER!

By Dave Carver

Prayer is intimate conversation with Jesus that seals our relationship and influences our lives—as we've seen in the Bible, in other people's lives, and in our own circumstances. Prayer, just like everything else in a relationship, must be learned. Even Jesus' disciples needed to learn how to communicate intimately with their Savior.

As youth leaders, we can guide students in their understanding of prayer, modeling how to pray, interceding for others, and creating situations that enable them to pray.

Use this lesson to help students understand prayer and to provide an opportunity for them to grow in prayer.

OBJECTIVES

In this lesson, kids will:

- explore their priorities,
- see examples of prayers in the Bible,
- list things they want to talk to Jesus about, and
- compose a group prayer.

THE LESSON

Take It Or Leaf It

(For each person, you'll need a pencil and a copy of the "Take It or Leaf It" handout on page 90.)

After students arrive, give everyone a pencil and a "Take It or Leaf It" handout. Say: **You have a drawing of a simple leaf. This leaf—like all others— depends on a complex network of veins to distribute nutrients throughout it. All living things have some sort of system to "keep them going." Let's talk for a few minutes about what keeps us going.**

Point out the leaf's primary veins. Have students each write on the veins the four or five most important things in their lives—things that keep them going. For example, someone might write, "music, a good relationship with parents, and the youth group."

When everyone's finished, have students share some of their responses. As students share, ask why they chose those items.

Prayer Song

(For each pair, you'll need a copy of the "One Person's Song" handout on page 91 and a pencil.)

Say: **Today we'll look at something that's a priority for me and really keeps me going: prayer. The Bible tells us that Jesus communicates with us through our prayers, and is moved by them. Let's take a deeper look at this.**

Form pairs, and give each pair a "One Person's Song" handout and a pencil. Say: **Please read this song someone wrote, and then answer the questions with your partner.**

After pairs discuss the questions, call everyone together and review the answers as a group. Ask a few people to explain why they chose their answers. Say: **The prayer you read is from Psalm 42 in the Bible. It shows that God wants us to pray and be honest about how we feel.**

Prayer Roles

3

(You'll need a copy of "A Prayer Pair" handout on page 92. Beforehand, cut apart the handout and assign the parts to two "dramatic" students. Have them be prepared to read their parts during this activity.)

Say: **Let's look at two more examples of prayer from the Bible.**

Introduce the first actor, the Religious Person. Have that person act out the character with great relish and enthusiasm.

Without pausing to reflect, say: **That's one model. Now let's look at another. Have the second actor, the Nerd, act out his or her prayer.**

Explain that this skit is based on a Bible passage. Ask someone to read aloud Luke 18:10-14. Ask:

- **What are some differences between these prayers?**
- **When have you been in each role, and how has that affected your relationship with Jesus?**
- **What can we learn about prayer from this activity?**

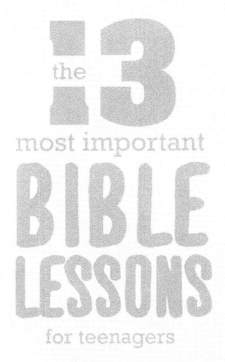

4 Prayer Lists

(You'll need markers and a whiteboard, or newsprint and tape. For each person, you'll need a sheet of paper and a pencil.)

On the board, number 1 through 10 from top to bottom. Say: **We've talked a lot about other people talking to Jesus. What about you? If you had the opportunity to talk with Jesus about anything, what would it be? Let's list 10 things we'd like to discuss with Jesus.**

List the suggestions as students give them. Examples might be "Why is there suffering?"; "Why do my parents fight so much?"; or "What do you want me to do with my life?" Don't discuss the suggestions; just list them.

When the list is complete, read aloud Philippians 4:6-7. Say: **Thinking about items like this can make us afraid, but Jesus promises that if we ask him to help us, his peace will protect us from fear.**

Give students each a sheet of paper and a pencil. Have them each write five concerns they'd like to ask Jesus to help them with and five things they're thankful for. When students are finished, say: **Take your list home, and tape it to your bathroom mirror. Pray each morning, asking for Jesus' help in those areas and thanking him for what he's done and continues to do in your life.**

Spinning Thanks

(No supplies needed.)

Say: **Often when people pray, they fold their hands or perhaps hold hands. As we prepare to leave, we'll pray in a couple of new ways. First, we'll thank God for one another.**

Have students form a circle and put their arms around one another. Say: **As we're linked together, we'll walk around to the left until someone says, "Stop." Then that person will say one thing he or she is thankful for about someone else in the room. For example, someone might say, "I'm thankful for Ben's sense of humor" or "I'm thankful Cara is such a good listener." Then we'll walk to the right until someone else says, "Stop." Each person can be mentioned only once. We'll continue until everyone has been mentioned.**

Closing Prayers

(You'll need a marker and a whiteboard, or newsprint and tape. For each person, you'll need a copy of the "Seven Tips for Prayer" handout on page 93.)

Have students stay in the circle with arms linked. Write "Dear Lord" on the board. Say: **Let's take a moment to talk to God about our time here. I've started the prayer. Let's all finish it. We'll go around the circle and have each person add a phrase to the prayer.** If you have time, have students each share two or three times.

Allow the group a minute or so to think, and, if necessary, provide a "jump start" by suggesting words such as "give," "tell," or "show."

After the prayer, give everyone a "Seven Tips for Prayer" handout to use at home.

TAKE IT OR LEAF IT

Every leaf—every being—has something that "keeps it going."

What keeps you going? What are some things that are important to you?

Is it music? sports? friends? your own car?

Think of four or five important things in your life, and write them on the veins of the leaf below.

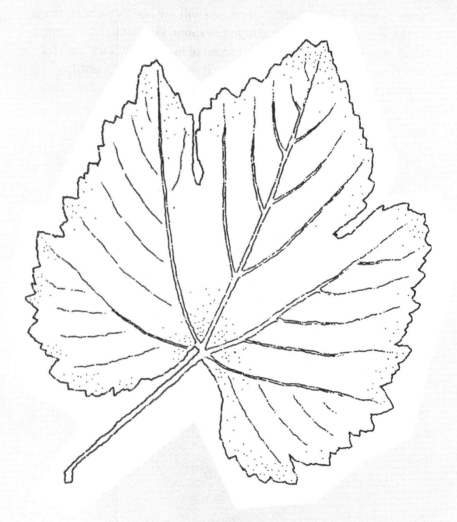

ONE PERSON'S SONG

Read this song carefully, and then answer the questions below.
You won't have to share your answers (although you'll have the opportunity), so be honest.

As the deer pants for streams of water, so my soul pants for you, O God. My soul thirsts for God, for the living God. When can I go and meet with God? My tears have been my food day and night, while men say to me all day long, "Where is your God?"

These things I remember as I pour out my soul: how I used to go with the multitude, leading the procession to the house of God, with shouts of joy and thanksgiving among the festive throng.

Why are you downcast, O my soul? Why so disturbed within me? Put your hope in God, for I will yet praise him, my Savior and my God. *

After you read the song, answer these questions:

1 Is this a prayer? Why or why not?

2 At the beginning of the song, how does the person feel about God? What are his emotions?

3 What change in emotions occurs by the end of the song? How can you tell?

4 What's one thing you've felt sad about in your relationship with Jesus?

5 Why is it important to pray? Why is it sometimes difficult to pray?

*Scripture taken from Psalm 42.

A PRAYER PAIR

Copy and cut apart these prayers.

PRAYER 1 — Religious Person

You're one of the most important people in your community, and everyone (including you) knows it. You have a reserved seat at church, and you're one of its largest contributors. You know that Jesus loves you—who wouldn't? You pray every now and then, and you're sure that Jesus looks forward to each occasion just to hear the sound of your voice.

With this in mind, dramatize the prayer below. Feel free to "ham it up"!

"Dear Jesus, I thank you that I'm not like other people. I'm not like the drug dealers, the cheaters, or even that nerd over there. Jesus, you know how much I do for you—all the contributions and everything. I'm glad we're on the same team, Jesus. Amen."

PRAYER 2—Nerd

You're one of the least-popular people in town, and everyone (including you) knows it. You don't really pray much, mostly because you don't feel worthy to talk to Jesus. You don't know what to think about yourself, but you know you need Jesus a lot more than he needs you.

With this in mind, dramatize the prayer below.

"Oh, Jesus, please listen to me. I know I haven't done much to deserve your help lately, but I believe in your promise to love me. I'm sorry for the wrong I've done. Help me do better tomorrow. Amen."

SEVEN TIPS FOR PRAYER

There are about as many ways to pray as there are people. What works for me might not work for you or for cousin Fred. Here are some hints that may help you in your prayer life. But remember: The best way to be a better "pray-er" is to practice!

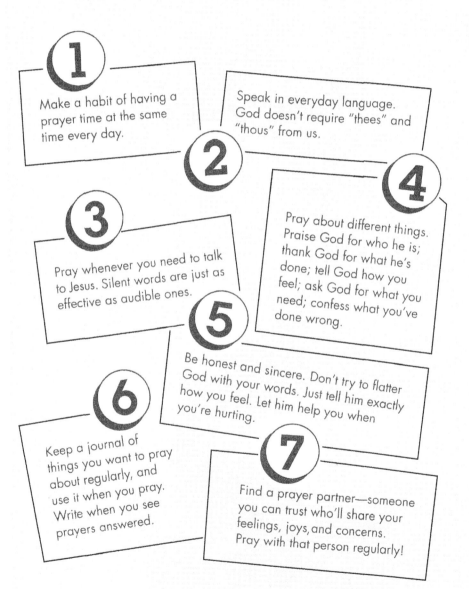

1 Make a habit of having a prayer time at the same time every day.

2 Speak in everyday language. God doesn't require "thees" and "thous" from us.

3 Pray whenever you need to talk to Jesus. Silent words are just as effective as audible ones.

4 Pray about different things. Praise God for who he is; thank God for what he's done; tell God how you feel; ask God for what you need; confess what you've done wrong.

5 Be honest and sincere. Don't try to flatter God with your words. Just tell him exactly how you feel. Let him help you when you're hurting.

6 Keep a journal of things you want to pray about regularly, and use it when you pray. Write when you see prayers answered.

7 Find a prayer partner—someone you can trust who'll share your feelings, joys, and concerns. Pray with that person regularly!

the 13

most important

BIBLE LESSONS

for teenagers

SHARING JESUS

By Scott C. Noon

During Jesus' life, he emphasized preaching about God's love and teaching others about him. Paul and the other apostles also affirmed the importance of telling others about Jesus as they began the church and invited people to believe. With the Holy Spirit's help and guidance, people continue to share Jesus and his love.

Although different strategies exist for exactly how to share Jesus, the important thing is to share him. Empowering young people to tell others about their faith is vital to their growth in Christ.

Use this lesson to help teenagers understand the importance of talking about their faith and discover effective ways to do it.

OBJECTIVES

In this lesson, students will:

- explore why it's sometimes hard to talk about their faith,
- understand the biblical command to share the gospel message,
- see how Jesus has been a part of their past and present, and
- identify simple ways of talking about their faith in Jesus with other people.

THE LESSON

Candy for All

(For each person, you'll need a piece of candy.)

As students arrive, give every other person a piece of candy but tell them not to eat it. When everyone arrives, tell the students with candy that you expect them to give it away to someone else. See what happens.

Some students will give away their candy. Others will refuse. Still others will trade candy with someone else who also has one. After the experience, ask:

- How did you feel when I told the candy-holders to give away their treats?
- Why did some people not want to give away their treat?
- How is this experience like sharing your faith in Jesus with others?

Say: Having faith in Jesus is like having a tasty treat we can share with others. But sometimes we hesitate to share because we're afraid we'll be embarrassed or rejected or stereotyped or ignored. Jesus gives us the strength to overcome our fears and share him with others.

Give candy to people who don't have any, and let everyone enjoy the treats.

Laying a Foundation

(You'll need markers and a whiteboard, or three sheets of newsprint and tape. You'll also need three balloons, each with one of these Bible references written on it: Matthew 28:19-20; Matthew 9:35-38; and Matthew 4:19. For each group of three, you'll need a Bible, a marker, and a copy of the "Faith Foundations" handout on page 101.)

Form groups of three. Give each group a Bible, a marker, and a "Faith Foundations" handout. Across the whiteboard or above each sheet of newsprint, tape the balloons that have Scripture references written on them.

Have groups work together to match the three statements on the handout with the correlating Bible verses on the balloons. As groups finish, have them write each statement under the reference they think it matches. When groups are finished, discuss any differences between the answers. Then read the Bible passages and give the correct answers. Here are the statements and corresponding Bible references:

- Jesus commands his followers to tell others about him (Matthew 28:19-20).
- The love Jesus has shown us motivates us to tell others about him (Matthew 9:35-38).
- Part of following Jesus means telling others about him (Matthew 4:19).

Faith Map

(For each person, you'll need a sheet of paper and several different-color markers.)

Say: **We all come to church because someone in our past told us about his or her faith. Let's think about the ways Jesus has been part of our lives in the past.**

Give everyone a sheet of paper and several markers. Have students draw a faith map—a timeline beginning with their birthdate and moving to the present. Be sure they include today's date on the right end of the time line. Have young people each "chart" their life of faith by indicating "highs" (when they felt particularly close to God) and "lows" (when they felt alone in the world), indicating what was happening to them. Be sure they mark life-changing events that affected their faith.

If some students don't have a relationship with Jesus, have them indicate other kinds of "highs" and "lows" on their timeline, such as an award or an extended illness.

After maps are complete, form groups of four. Have students take turns explaining their map to everyone, describing how they came to the place they are today.

Retelling the Story

(No supplies needed.)

After students tell their stories, have them answer these questions in their groups:

- **How did you come to know God? Was it quick and all at once or slow and over time?**
- **Who shared the message of Jesus with you—and how?**

Afterward, call everyone together. Say: **We effectively tell others about Jesus when we combine three important elements: who Jesus is, our own story of life with Jesus, and the circumstances of the person we're talking to.**

Have students get back into their groups of three, and ask groups to quickly role-play one of the following situations. It's okay if more than one group has the same role play. Have one person act as the person in need and the other two help that person by telling their own faith stories. Move the groups quickly so the skits aren't too complex.

Situation #1

Two Christian friends are talking to a non-Christian friend whose boyfriend just broke up with her.

Situation #2

Two Christian friends are talking to a non-Christian friend who's failing three classes in school.

Situation #3

Two Christian friends are talking to a non-Christian friend whose parents just kicked him out of the house.

Have groups take turns presenting their skits to everyone. Afterward, ask:

- **How did it feel to tell your own faith story in your skit?**
- **What made these situations seem real?**
- **What makes telling your faith most effective?**

Clothespin Closings

(You'll need a piece of string long enough to stretch across your meeting room. For each person, you'll need three wooden clothespins or plastic clips and a marker.)

Say: **Each of us is unique in Jesus' eyes. Many people who hold a special place in our hearts don't know Jesus yet. Let's close by praying for them specifically.**

Give students each three wooden clothespins or plastic clips, and a marker. Have them write the names of three people they want to tell about Jesus (one per clothespin or clip).

Tie a string across the room so it resembles a clothesline. Have students come up one at a time and clip one clothespin on the string, then say a one- or two-sentence prayer that Jesus will help them share their faith effectively. Continue until each person has prayed three times. Close by thanking Jesus for hearing our prayers.

FAITH FOUNDATIONS

Match these statements with the Scriptures listed on the balloons.

Jesus commands his followers to

tell others about him.

The love Jesus has shown us motivates us
to tell others about him.

Part of following Jesus means telling
others about him.

the 13

most important

BIBLE
LESSONS

for teenagers

FAITH IN ACTION

By Karen Ceckowski

The challenge to serve other people resounds clearly throughout the Bible. Jesus gives countless examples of service and calls us to do likewise. The opportunity to put faith into action opens new doors of understanding and growth for adults and young people alike.

Teenagers who learn the value of serving discover new dimensions in their faith. They see there's more to life on earth than just fulfilling their own needs and desires.

Use this lesson to help students see how serving others imitates Jesus and brings them closer to him.

OBJECTIVES

In this lesson, students will:

- respond to how it feels to be served,
- evaluate how much time they spend serving others,
- identify people who need help,
- discuss why Jesus calls us to serve, and
- commit to a service project.

THE LESSON

Serving the Masses

(You'll need soothing music and a music player, snacks, and drinks.)

As students enter, have them get comfortable. Play soothing music in the background. Serve students snacks and drinks. Be kind and courteous, going out of your way to talk to everyone. After you've talked to each person, turn off the music and ask:

- How did it feel to be served as you came in?
- How would you rate my service from 1 to 10, with 10 being best? Why?
- What made this service special or unusual?
- Within the last 24 hours, and not counting my service to you right now, when is the last time someone served one of your needs? What did they do?

Scheduled to Serve

(For each person, you'll need a copy of the "Time to Serve" handout on page 109 and a pencil.)

Give each person a "Time to Serve" handout and a pencil. Have students complete the handout by writing what their typical week's activities include. For example, in one week students might spend:

- 35 hours in school,
- 10 hours doing homework,
- 1 hour in worship,
- 2 hours at youth group,
- 8 hours eating,
- 60 hours sleeping,
- 25 hours on social media,
- 25 hours watching shows or playing games,
- 3 hours hanging out with friends,
- 3 hours with a boyfriend or girlfriend, and
- 1 hour talking with parents.

After everyone's list is complete, draw an imaginary line down the middle of the room. Explain that one end of the room represents zero hours and the other end of the room represents the entire week—168 hours. Have students total the hours they spent doing something for someone else in the last week (schoolwork doesn't count). Have them stand on the spot of the line that represents that amount of hours. Ask a few people to share what they did to serve others.

Next, have students total the hours other people spent serving them in the last week. Have students stand on the spot of the line that represents that amount of hours. Ask how others served them.

Say: **It's good for us to know how we spend our time. Today we'll explore the topic of serving and the role it plays in our daily lives as followers of Jesus.**

Progressive Play

(You'll need a marker and a whiteboard, or newsprint and tape.)

Write these conditions on the board:

- hungry
- poor
- depressed
- helpless
- sick
- imprisoned
- lonely

Ask two young people to be actors, and number them 1 and 2. Have the rest of the group work together to decide these parameters:

- Location (must be outside),
- Time of year,
- Relationship between the two people (friends, brothers, husband and wife, etc.), and
- Subject of conversation (you judge whether the suggested subjects are appropriate).

Explain that the actors will be doing an improvisational skit about the conditions listed on the board, and everyone else will be directors. Tell the actors that every 30 seconds during the performance, you or another director will call out an actor's number and a new condition from the list, such as "#1—poor" or "#2— lonely." That actor must immediately assume that condition without stopping the skit. To begin, assign actor #1 as hungry and actor #2 as depressed.

Have the actors assume their roles and start talking. Every 30 seconds, have a different director change an actor's condition. Continue until each actor has changed conditions three or four times. Make sure the skit covers all the conditions.

After the skit, congratulate the actors and directors on their performance. Say: **We laughed through this skit, but each condition the actors portrayed is serious and sad. Let's think about how we can serve other people who face these problems.**

Examine the Possibilities

(You'll need a Bible, a marker, and a whiteboard, or newsprint and tape.)

Have students brainstorm practical ways they can serve people who are facing the situations covered in the skit. Write responses on the board. Encourage students to think of things they can actually do.

After students share, say: **These service ideas would make people feel special and meet needs in their lives. But they'd also take up time we might want to spend doing other things.**

Ask:

- **What have you sacrificed in order to serve someone else?**

Read aloud Matthew 25:31-46. Ask:

- **Why does Jesus want us to serve other people?**

5 Media Service

(You'll need magazines.)

Distribute magazines. Have students sit in a circle, thumb through the magazines, and read the ads. Go around the circle and let students each tell about the services offered by one of the ads. For example, a car ad may offer dependability, a smooth ride, comfortable seating, or an affordable price.

After everyone has a turn, ask:

- Would the services you listed from your ad convince you to buy the product? Why or why not?
- How are the services offered in these ads the same as or different from the kinds of services we listed earlier?

Say: TV and magazine ads would have us believe we can serve ourselves and be happy and content for the rest of our lives, but we know that isn't true. True service that really makes a difference in our lives goes much deeper.

6 I Choose to Serve

(You'll need the service list from activity 4. For each person, you'll need an index card and a pencil.)

Give students each an index card and a pencil. Have them each choose one service project to work on. It can be one from the list created in activity 4 or a new one they think of.

Say: On your card, write what you're going to do. Make it specific and include a completion date.

Service Sharing

(You'll need a Bible, a sheet of paper, and a pencil.)

Form a circle, and have students take turns sharing their service project. Read aloud James 2:14-18. Close by asking Jesus to bless students' acts of service.

Encourage students to keep their cards as a reminder to serve. Write down each person's name and service project. Check in with students down the road and encourage them to keep their commitments.

TIME TO SERVE

In the chart below, write all the things you do in a week and how much time you spend doing each one. Remember, each week has 168 hours.

Activity	Hours Spent

the 13

most important

BIBLE
LESSONS

for teenagers

ETERNITY WITH JESUS

By Lin Johnson

Teenagers want answers about the future. They want to know what they'll do after high school and college, who they'll marry, what kind of job they'll have, how much money they'll make, and so on. They also want to know what will happen to them when they die, how the world will end, and what heaven and hell are like.

Many young people fear what's ahead, including violence, ecological disaster, war, economic instability, disease, overpopulation and more. They need to hear Jesus' assurances about the future, offered in his Word.

Use this lesson to share with teenagers what Jesus tells us about the future and to encourage them to respond to Jesus' invitation to spend their future with him.

OBJECTIVES

In this lesson, students will:

- illustrate people's preoccupation with the future,
- explain four aspects of the End Times,
- discover what heaven and hell are like, and
- respond to Jesus' invitation to spend the future with him.

THE LESSON

Newspaper Montage

(You'll need newspapers. For each group of three or four, you'll need scissors, tape, and a large sheet of paper.)

As students arrive, direct them each to make a newspaper montage. Form groups of three or four. Have students look through the newspapers and cut or tear out anything that deals with the future: articles, headlines, predictions, movie ads, ads for personal readings or horoscopes, and so on. Instruct groups to tape these to their paper.

When groups are finished, have them each choose a spokesperson to show their montage.

Ask:

- **What fascinates or excites you the most about the future?**
- **What scares you the most about the future?**

Say: **Most people are interested in the future, but none of us knows what'll happen. The Bible tells us some things we can know for sure, though. Today we'll explore four specific future events.**

Future Newscast

(You'll need a copy of the "Future Features" handout on page 115, paper, and pencils.)

Form four newscast teams. Give teams each a section of the "Future Features" handout, paper, and pencils. Have teams each read their Scripture and prepare a newscast segment on their subject. They can do a news story reporting the facts, an opinion or editorial feature, an interview, or any other kind of segment on a newscast. Encourage students to be creative, but make sure they don't change the facts. The whole team must participate. Students can act as newscasters and field reporters, and they can also be props such as a desk or a microphone.

When teams are ready, have them take turns presenting the segments. Applaud each team's efforts, and take time for any questions students have as a result of the presentations. Then ask:

- How did you feel as you listened to the newscasts, and why?
- From this activity, what's something new you learned about the future?
- How can this information affect the way you live now?

Future Endings

(No supplies needed.)

Say: **Jesus tells us that after we die, we'll spend eternity in one of two places: heaven or hell. We know heaven is a wonderful place—beyond comprehension! But what will it be like for people who go to hell?**

Have students form a circle. Walk around the circle and pull out every fourth person. Then have students in the circle give one another back rubs while the other students watch. If the other students try to give back rubs, don't allow it. Instead, say: **You can't have one. You have to be in the circle to get a back rub.**

After about a minute, ask the people who didn't get back rubs:

- What was it like to be left out?
- How is this similar to or different from being "left out" of heaven?

Have the rest of the students give one another backrubs. Say: **Being left out of this experience was bad, but once you die, there are no second chances to get to heaven.**

Invitation From Jesus

(For each person, you'll need a Bible and a copy of the "Jesus' Invitation" handout on page 116.)

Read aloud John 14:3. Say: **Jesus wants each of us to spend eternity with him in heaven. He doesn't want to be separated from us forever.**

Give students each a "Jesus' Invitation" handout. Let students read the front. Then explain Christ's gift of eternal life listed on the inside, explaining and expanding as necessary. Have a few students read aloud the Scripture.

RSVP

(For each person, you'll need a pencil and the copies of the "Jesus' Invitation" handout from activity 4.)

Give students each a pencil. Have students read the "RSVP" page from the "Jesus' Invitation" handout, respond by checking the appropriate box, and write their names on the invitation. Then collect the invitations so you can follow up with individuals later. Invite students to talk with you after the lesson if they want to accept Jesus' invitation now or would like more information.

Future Blessings

(No supplies needed.)

Have students form a circle. Say: **Turn to the person on your right and say, "I want to spend the future in heaven with you because...."** **Complete the sentence with a positive remark.**

Have students go around the circle until everyone has completed the sentence.

Close with prayer, thanking Jesus for not leaving us guessing about the future and for wanting to spend eternity with us.

FUTURE FEATURES

Copy and cut apart these sections.

Heaven and Hell

Matthew 25:41, 46

Revelation 20:10

Revelation 21:4

Revelation 22:3, 5

Jesus' Coming

John 14:1-3

Acts 1:9-11

1 Thessalonians 4:15-17

Judgment

Of believers in Jesus:
Romans 14:10-12
2 Corinthians 5:10

Of people who don't believe in Jesus:
John 3:17-18
Revelation 20:11-15

End of the World

2 Peter 3:10-13

Revelation 21:1-4

JESUS' INVITATION

Copy, cut out, and fold an invitation for each person.

Jesus says...

- I love you and want you to have eternal life (John 3:16).
- However, you're a sinner, and your sin has separated you from me. Death is the penalty for your sin (Romans 3:23; 6:23a).
- But I have paid the penalty for your sin (Romans 5:8).
- To have eternal life, you must put your faith in me only (Ephesians 2:8-9).
- Once you do so, you can never lose your eternal life (1 John 5:13).

RSVP

- [ ] I've already accepted Jesus' invitation.
- [ ] Yes, I accept Jesus' invitation now.
- [ ] I need more time to think about it.
- [ ] I'm undecided but would like to talk about it.

fold first

You're invited!

Spend the future with me.

fold second